Benjamin Victor

The History of the Theatres of London

From the Year 1760 to the Present Time

Benjamin Victor

The History of the Theatres of London
From the Year 1760 to the Present Time

ISBN/EAN: 9783743393912

Manufactured in Europe, USA, Canada, Australia, Japa

Cover: Foto ©ninafisch / pixelio.de

Manufactured and distributed by brebook publishing software (www.brebook.com)

Benjamin Victor

The History of the Theatres of London

THE HISTORY

OF THE

THEATRES OF LONDON,

From the Year 1760 to the present Time.

BEING

A Continuation of the ANNUAL REGISTER of all the new Tragedies, Comedies, Farces, Pantomimes, &c. that have been performed within that Period.

WITH

Occasional NOTES and ANECDOTES.

By MR. VICTOR,

AUTHOR of the two former VOLUMES.

LONDON:
Printed for T. BECKET, in the Strand.
MDCCLXXI.

TO
MRS. BOOTH.

Madam,

TO whom can this third Volume of the *History of the Theatres* be addrefs'd, with more Propriety, than to one who fo early in Life (above half a Century ago) made fo agreeable a Figure there! And yet I know you had rather pafs your remaining Days forgotten as an Actrefs, than to have your Youth recollected in the moft favourable Light: But I hope you will excufe the Liberty I take, in commemorating the Delight which the Public received from your Performances, while you was an Ornament to the Theatre! for the Proof of which I can turn to Records more confiderable than my own, and find in Mr. Colley Cibber's Apology for his Life, the following remarkable Paffage, (Page 347.)

> " But during the Trial of *Sa-cheverel* our Audiences were extremely weakened by the better Rank of people's attending it; while, at the fame time, the lower Sort as eagerly crouded into *Drury-lane* Theatre, to a new Comedy called the *Fair Quaker of Deal.* This Play having
> " fome

" some low Strokes of natural
" Humour, was rightly calcu-
" lated for the Capacity of the
" Actors who play'd in it; but
" the most happy Incident in
" its Fortune was the Charm
" of the *Fair Quaker*, which
" was acted by MISS SANT-
" LOW (afterwards Mrs. *Booth)*
" whose Person was then in the
" full Bloom of what Beauty
" she could pretend to: Before
" this she had only been ad-
" mired as the most excellent
" Dancer; which, perhaps,
" might not a little contribute
" to the favourable Reception
" she met with as an Actress
" in

" in this Character, which so
" happily suited her Figure and
" Capacity:—The gentle Soft-
" ness of her Voice—the com-
" posed Innocence of her As-
" pect—the Modesty of her
" Dress—the reserved Decency
" of her Gesture, and the Sim-
" plicity of the Sentiments
" that naturally fell from her—
" made her seem the amiable
" Maid she represented: In a
" Word, not the enthusiastick
" Maid of *Orleans* was more
" serviceable of old to the
" *French* Army, when the
" *English* had distress'd them,
" than this *Fair Quaker* was,
" at the Head of that Dramatic
" Attempt,

" Attempt, upon which the
" Support of their weak So-
" ciety depended."

Thus, Madam, by this Account, your Powers began to break forth at firſt, in no ſmall Degree of Luſtre as an Actreſs! having ſome Years before charm'd the admiring Public as the moſt elegant Dancer! It was therefore no Wonder that Mr. *Booth*, the moſt conſiderable Man in the Theatre, ſhould become a Lover! which ſoon appear'd in the following inſpired Ode written by him on your Dancing.

" She comes! the God of Love afferts his Reign,
" Refiftlefs o'er the gazing Throng!
" Alone fhe fills the fpacious Scene!
" The Charm of ev'ry Eye! the Praife of ev'ry
" Tongue!

" Order and Grace together join'd,
" Sweetnefs with Majefty combin'd,
" To make the beauteous Form compleat,
" On ev'ry Step and Motion wait.

" Now, to a flow and melting Air fhe moves!
" Her Eyes their Softnefs fteal from *Venus*'
" Doves!
" So like in Shape, in Air, and Mien,
" She paffes for the *Paphian* Queen!
" The Graces all around her play;
" The wond'ring Gazers die away.

" But now, the flying Fingers ftrike the Lyre!
" The fprightlier Notes the Nymph infpire!
" She whirls around! fhe bounds! fhe fprings!
" As if *Jove*'s Meffenger had lent her Wings!
" Such

" Such *Daphne* was, when near old *Peneus*'
"   Stream
"   She fled to shun a loath'd Embrace!
" (Of antient Bards the frequent Theme)
" Such were her lovely Limbs, so flush'd her
"   charming Face!

" So round her Neck, her Eyes so fair!
" So rose her swelling Chest, so flow'd her am-
"   ber Hair!
"   While her swift Feet outstripp'd the Wind,
"   And left th' enamour'd God of Day be-
"   hind.

"   While the light-footed Fairy flies,
"   Our mounting Spirits nimbly rise!
"   The Pulse still answers to the Strains,
"   And the Blood dances in our Veins.
"   Of *Cynthia*'s Air let Poets dream,
"   When from the hoary Mountain's Height,
"   Down to *Eurota*'s silent Stream
" She leads her Virgin Train, and charms the
"   Sight!
                                        " Whether

" Whether on Mountains, or in Woods,
" In flow'ry Lawns or verdant Fields,
" Or bathing in the silver Floods,
" Lo! to a mortal Fair the fancy'd Goddess
" yields!"

Some Time after, this accomplished Lover became an Husband; and, to his Death, one of the most affectionate that ever Woman was blessed with! To that I can bear witness—as I often reflect with Pleasure, that, at so early a Part of my Life, I had the Happiness of being distinguished by the Friendship of a Man of his exalted Merit—descended from a noble Family—a Scholar, and a Gentleman—and not only the first in his Profession, but, at that Period, even without the Shadow of a Rival!

At

At his lamented Death, in the Year 1733, you prudently retired from the public Eye; and have enjoyed a long exemplary Life of Widowhood, with that Serenity, and Elegance, as would have done Honour to any Rank or any Profeſſion!

Permit me, Madam, to congratulate you on the laſt Proof of your good Senſe and Gratitude, *(viz.)* your determin'd Reſolution to erect a Monument to the lov'd Memory of Mr. *Booth*.

I am,
(With the greateſt Reſpect)
Madam,
Your moſt obliged Friend,
and Servant,

London,
23d *March*, 1771.

HISTORICAL REGISTER

OF THE

THEATRES ROYAL.

IN my Second Volume of the History of the Theatres, the Register of the *new performances* is brought down to the Year 1760; the Dramatic Novelties of the Season terminate with the Approach of the annual Benefits, which always commence about the Middle of *March* :—On the 28th of that Month died Mrs. MARGARET WOFFINGTON, at the Age of Forty-two.

Her natural Vivacity added to her elegant Form, were admirably suited to the higher

higher Characters in Comedy.——*Lady Betty Modish—Lady Townly—Maria* in the *Nonjuror*, &c.—This Truth was also confirmed by her great Success in the Character of *Sir Harry Wildair*; where she appeared with the true Spirit of a wellbred Rake of Quality! and after the Death of the celebrated original Mr. Wilks, she remained the unrivalled *Wildair* during her Life.

I know many Critics would not admit of her Powers for Tragedy:—Her Voice was not harmonized for the plaintive Notes of Sorrow;—besides, they said, she had been at *Paris*, and adopted the Air and Manner of the famous *Madame Dumesnil*, which appeared too affected, and extravagant for an English Audience—Yet, with great Deference to their superior Judgment, her Performance of *Andromache* was much

much admired, where the true Spirit of the noble Grecian Matron, was forcibly and elegantly supported!—I could mention other Characters in Tragedy in which she commanded Applause; but, at the same Time it must be acknowledged, her Genius was superior in Comedy.

It was the Fashion to follow this celebrated Actress, and applaud her in a very particular Manner, whenever she appeared in the Character of *Sir Harry Wildair*; the Approbation was not merely the Whim of the Winter, but it remained, and continued as long as she chose to represent that Character; and it must be confessed to her Praise as an Actress, that the Ease, Manner of Address, Vivacity, and Figure of a young Man of Fashion was never more happily exhibited: The best Proof of this Matter is the well known Success

Success and Profit, she brought to the different Theatres in *England* and *Ireland*, whenever her Name was published for *Sir Harry Wildair*; the Managers always had recourse to this Lady for this Character, whenever they had Fears of the Want of an Audience; and, indeed, for some Years before she died, as she never, by her Articles, was to play it but with her own Consent, she always conferred a Favour upon the Managers whenever she changed her Sex, and filled their Houses.

At her first Appearance in *England*, the following Lines were addressed to her——

To Mrs. WOFFINGTON,
appearing in the Part of *Silvia* in the
Recruiting Officer.

" When first in Petticoats you trod the Stage,
" Our Sex with Love you fir'd, your own with Rage!

" In

"In Breeches next; so well you play'd the Cheat,
"The pretty Fellow, and the Rake compleat—
"Each Sex, were then, with different Passions mov'd,
"The Men grew envious, and the Women loved."

However, the Difficulty of a Woman appearing in Man's Cloaths is much less, and more common, than the same Woman appearing as a real Man.

And now, ye fair ones of the Stage, it will not be foreign to the Subject, to consider whether it is proper for you (notwithstanding the great Reputation Mrs. *Woffington* acquired in acting *Sir Harry Wildair*) to perform the Characters of Men.

I will venture in the Name of all sober, discreet, sensible, Spectators *(the Censure of one of which, must, in your Opinion, outweigh a whole Theatre of others)* to answer, No! there is something required so much beyond the Delicacy of your Sex, to arrive at the Point of Perfection, that, if you hit it, you may be condemned as a Woman, and if you do not, you are injured as an *Actress*.

In the first Place, supposing you are formed in Mind and Body (and it is supposing a great deal) like the Actress in Question—for she had Beauty, Shape, Wit, and Vivacity, equal to any theatrical Female in any Time, and capable of any Undertaking in the Province of Comedy, nay of deceiving, and warming into Passion, any of her own Sex, if she had been unknown, and introduced as a young Baronet just returned from his Travels—but still, I say, admirable and admired as she was in this Part, I would not have any other Female of the Stage attempt the Character after her; the wearing Breeches merely to pass for a Man, as is the Case in many Comedies,

Comedies, is as far as the Metamorphosis ought to go, and indeed, more than some formal Critics will allow of; but that Custom is established into a Law, and as there is great Latitude in it, it should not be in the least extended—when it is, you *o'erstep the Modesty of Nature*, and when that is done, whatever may be the Applause within Doors, you will be injured by Remarks and Criticisms without. The following Lines of *Pope*, may be properly applied to the Subject.

> " In all, let *Nature* never be forgot—
> " But treat the Goddess like a modest Fair,
> " Nor over dress, nor leave her wholly bare;
> " Let not each Beauty every where be spy'd,
> " Where half the Skill, is decently to hide."

The same Objections will hold to the Men assuming Womens Characters; each

Change becomes unnatural; and whenever a Man appears effeminate, or a Woman masculine, they will, in Spite of temporary Applause, be great Losers in the End.

THEATRE ROYAL
DRURY-LANE.

September 1760.

THE TEARS AND TRIUMPHS OF PARNASSUS. A Mafque, written by Mr. *Lloyd*, Author of a celebrated Poem, called the *Actor*—and fet to Mufic by Mr. *Stanley*. This Performance was an Elegy on the late King's Death, and an Elogium on the Acceffion of his prefent Majefty. Thefe little temporary Pieces, generally founded upon fome Allegory, are merely meant as Compliments from the Theatre,

and

and as such, generally pass off without much Observation.

October.

THE MINOR—a Farce of two Acts, by Mr. *Foote*. This Piece was performed with great Applause, but with still greater the preceeding Summer, at the little Theatre in the *Hay-Market*. —This Performance was a very proper Attack upon the Spirit of Fanaticism, which had risen to such a Height that it called for the Power of Satire, as it grew stronger by any Exertion of the Civil Power.

POLLY HONEYCOMB. A Farce of two Acts, by Mr. *Colman*. This was his first Attempt in the Dramatic Way: it met with Approbation the first Night—but as *Miss Pope* was a growing Favourite, and Mrs. *Kennedy* hit off the maudlin Character of Mrs. *Honeycomb*; this Farce improved nightly on the Audience, and became an established Entertainment. This was a very original Subject upon the Stage, and the pernicious Consequences of Novel reading, and imbibing Passions from such Books, was most humorously and properly exposed.

THE ENCHANTER, a Masque, supposed to be written by Mr. *Garrick*, set to Music by Mr. *Smith*, and performed with Success. This was written to shew to Advantage the fine Voice of *Lione*, a Jew Boy.—He is now much admired,

admired, and followed on particular Days at the Synagogue.

January 1761.

THE WAY TO KEEP HIM, by Mr. *Murphy*, a Comedy lengthened from three into five Acts.— Much improved and well received.

EDGAR AND EMELINE, a Fairy Tale, by Doctor *Hawkfworth*, performed several Nights with Applause. Mr. *Yates* and Mr. *O'Brien* were excellent in the two capital Characters.

February.

THE JEALOUS WIFE, a Comedy, by Mr. *Colman*, acted with Success. —It was observed by the greatest Connoisseurs, and those who remember the last Race of great Actors,

Actors, that no Scenes ever produced greater Effect than those in which Mrs. *Pritchard* and Mr. *Garrick* exerted their Comic Talents in the Characters of Mr. and Mrs. *Oakly*.

March.

ISLAND OF SLAVES — a Farce, translated from *Marivaux*, brought to the Stage by Mrs. *Clive*, for her own Benefit, and performed that Night only.

THE REGISTER OFFICE — a Farce of two Acts, by Mr. *Reed*.

This Author complained greatly of Injuries his Piece had received —He has hinted at some in his Preface :—The Subject is a good one, and capable of a great deal of Humour and useful Satire.

tire. It is a very agreeable Entertainment.

P. S. This Author has revised, and added a Character or two to this Farce, which has brought it into great Reputation.

COVENT-GARDEN THEATRE.

January 1761.

THE MARRIED LIBERTINE. A Comedy, by Mr. *Macklin*. This Comedy was violently oppofed the firft Night, but the Author (who performed the Character of the Married Libertine) had Addrefs enough to carry it nine Nights through a continued Oppofition.

THOMAS AND SALLY—A Ballad Farce, by Mr. *Bickerftaff*, fet to Mufic by Doctor *Arne*. The Songs were well fet, and well fung, and the Piece juftly applauded.

DRURY-LANE THEATRE.

October 1761.

ARCADIA, a Dramatic Pastoral, written in Honor of their Majesties Nuptials, by *Robert Lloyd*, A. M. Complimentary, and short lived.

HIGH LIFE BELOW STAIRS, a Farce of two Acts. Author unknown, though guessed at.

This Farce met with a little Opposition the first Night, from those whose Interest it was to oppose it:—But as very useful Satire was conveyed with true Humour, and met with general Appro-

Approbation—the Malecontents thought proper to withdraw their Oppofition, though they could not fubdue their Refentments; which broke out in a very particular Manner in other Places. In *Edinburgh*, when this Farce was acted there, the party-coloured Gentry collected themfelves into fo formidable a Body, that nothing but the fpirited affemblage of the Noblemen and Gentlemen could fupprefs! and the Confequence was an Association among them to deftroy that fcandalous Cuftom of giving *Vails to Servants*, which is the Practice of no other Nation; and which has been long the Difgrace of thefe Kingdoms, when vifited by Foreigners.

CYMBELINE, a Tragedy, written by SHAKESPEAR, with some little Alterations, by which the Stage is enriched with another excellent Play from that great Author.

December.

HECUBA, a Tragedy, by a Gentleman of *Cambridge*, acted three Nights—not ill treated—but neglected.—This Author might have taken the Hint from *Hamlet*, who said, (near two hundred Years ago) *What's Hecuba to Him, or He to Hecuba.* The Sentiments, and Diction of this Tragedy, evidently prove the Author was only unhappy in the Choice of his Subject.

January 1762.

THE DRUMMER, OR THE HAUNTED HOUSE, a Comedy, written by Mr. *Addison*.

This Comedy was brought to the Managers of *Drury-Lane* Theatre about the Year 1717, by Sir *Richard Steele*, who wrote a Preface to the printed Copy, where he owns it was not well received (though inimitably acted by all the great Comedians of those Days) or, at least, not so well as it deserved; which he accounts for by observing that the Strokes therein are too delicate for every Taste in a popular Assembly; and he adds that his Brother Sharers *(Cibber, Wilks,* and *Booth)* were of Opinion that it was like a Picture, in which the Strokes were not strong enough to appear at a Distance.

Mr. *Tickell*, who was appointed by his Friend Mr. *Addison* to publish a correct Edition of his Works after his Decease (which appeared in the Year 1721) omitted this Comedy; which Sir *Richard Steele* so much resented, that he caused a second Edition of the *Drummer* to be printed, with an Epistle to Mr. *Congreve*, wherein he enlarges warmly on the Merits of the Play, and declares it to be written by his late excellent Friend Mr. *Addison*. Upon this Declaration it was revived by Mr. *Rich*'s Company of Comedians in *Lincoln's-Inn-Fields*, and tho' much worse performed, was followed and greatly applauded.

From

From all this we may see the Power of Names, and Force of Fashion! but as the Influence of those great Names is now no more, the Reception of this Comedy from the *impartial Public* is very near what it at first met with. The Characters of *Vellum* and *Abigal* are admirably drawn, and so is that of *Tinsell* with true Humour—but the Scenes, in general, being rather languid in the Action for want of Business and Spirit, this Comedy, tho' it will not set the Theatre in bursts of Laughter, will by the chaste and admirable Representation of Nature, afford great Entertainment in the Closet.

The

The *Drummer* was revived at this Period at both Theatres, and confessedly allowed by a Prologue spoken at *Covent Garden* House (well suited to the silly Occasion) to take Advantage of the reigning Weakness of the People, who went in Crowds many Days and Nights to an *Haunted House*, by what was called the *Cock-Lane Ghost*—a Delusion set on foot, and very ingeniously carried on, by a Girl of twelve Years of Age, the Daughter of the Clerk of *St. Sepulchre*'s Church, who resided in *Cock-Lane* near *Smithfield*.

The Story of this Ghost was founded on the sudden Death of a young a young Woman, whose Name was *Fanny*, who lived some time before in that Family, and was the supposed Mistress of a Gentleman, who removed her from thence into a Lodging in *Clerkenwell*, where she died—and was buried in that Church.—— Her Ghost (which was reported to haunt this Girl by strange knockings and scratchings) was to insinuate that some foul Practices had been used to deprive her of Life; and to bring the Gentleman (as it did) into Trouble.

It would be incredible to relate the Numbers of Persons of Distinction that attended this Delusion! many of whom treated ed it as a serious and most important Affair; and though several very artful and proper Methods were tried to make the Discovery, they were for a long Time unsuccessful—at last—the Girl's Father, and three or four others were tried in the King's-Bench—found guilty—pilloried, and imprisoned. This most effectually laid the Ghost; and is the best and properest Cure for every Ghost that may arise hereafter.

THE SCHOOL FOR LOVERS, a *Comedy*, by *William Whitehead*, Esq. Poet Laureat.

This Piece is an agreeable Performance, and very interesting; it is of that Species of the Drama

Drama which has more of the Pathos than the Vis comica, and calculated more to draw Tears than raife Laughter. However, there are fome Scenes of Humor happily interwoven—It is faid, to be taken in Part from a Comedy of *Fontenelle*'s, called *Le Teſtament*.—Such is the School for Lovers—but with the matchlefs Powers of a *Garrick*, *Cibber*, and *Clive*, it was juftly applauded.

THE MUSICAL LADY, a *Farce* of two Acts, by *George Colman*, Efq.

This Farce was well acted, and well received.

THE FARMER RETURNED, a Dramatic Interlude. The writing and acting of that Character by Mr. *Garrick*, is another Inftance of his incomparable univerſal Genius.

This little Piece is a pleaſing Picture of a Farmer and his Family, to whom, on his Return from *London*, he gives a humorous Deſcription of the *Coronation*, and a ludricous Account of the Folly of the *Cock-Lane* Ghoſt juſt mentioned.—The Author's Friend, the late celebrated Mr. *Hogarth*, gave him a Sketch of his Pencil for the Frontiſpiece; and Mr. *Garrick*, in Return, dedicated this Interlude to him.

COVENT-GARDEN THEATRE.

September 1761.

SOON after the opening of this Season died Mr. *Lacy Ryan*, the oldest Actor in that, or any Company: He was a Tragedian of the first Consequence as to his cast of Parts (as *Hamlet, Richard,* &c.—and the fine Gentleman in most of the Comedies—but with extraordinary Singularities in all;) In his Tragedy tones, the Sound came to the Ear like that of a Man half strangled. As to his Qualifications for his Parts in Comedy, in his Person he was neither handsome or genteel; and yet by the Force of Custom, and long Habitude, something like Excellence was discovered in many of his Parts, particularly in *Ford* in the *Merry Wives of Windsor*.

Mr. *Ryan* was one of the young Actors that revolted from *Drury-Lane* Theatre to join the young Manager, Mr. *Rich*, in his new Government at his Theatre Royal in *Lincolns-Inn-Fields* about the Year 1716, under whose Management he died. Mr. *Ryan* was a Man of Sense and Spirit, and in private Life well respected.

Nothing new appeared in the first three Months at *Covent-Garden* Theatre; the Manager being employed in getting up a pompous *Coronation* suitable to the Times, his present *Majesty* having been just before crowned. Mr. *Rich* had a just Notion of the *public Spectacle*, viz. *That no Expence should be spared*—it should be *magnificent*

or

or *nothing*.—His ill Health (having been long afflicted with the Stone) and his accustomed Exactness in such like Exhibitions, delayed his Shew for some Time. —He died in the Run of it, in the Month of *December*, at the Age of Seventy Years.

The Father of this Gentleman was bred to the Law; and the first of the Name and Family that embarked in a Theatrical Government; his Abilities for that undertaking, are fully set forth by Mr. *Cibber* sen. in his Apology for his Life, who was well acquainted with them.—He opens the 8th Chapter of his Book as follows:

" Though the Master of our Theatre
" had no Conception himself of Theatri-
" cal Merit, either in Authors or Actors,
" yet his Judgement was governed by a
" saving Rule in both.—He looked into
" his

"his Receipts for the Value of a Play,
"and from common Fame he judged of
"his Actors."

But his Son, the late Manager, who had continued in that Office without a Partner above Forty Years, had very useful Abilities as a Performer in Pantomimes, under the feigned Name of *Lun!* and his excellence as an *Harlequin* deserves a Place in the Records of the Theatre. He was the Inventor of the *English* Harlequin, which is a quite different Character from that of the *Italian*. Whatever he undertook to describe to the Audience was as clearly and fully understood, as Words added to the Action of others could express.—To confirm this Opinion I shall here quote the following Lines from a Prologue written by Mr. *Garrick* to an

Enter-

Entertainment in which was a speaking Harlequin,

" But why a speaking Harlequin? 'tis wrong,
" The Wits will say to give the Fool a Tongue:
" When *Lun* appear'd, with matchless Art and
" Whim,
" He gave the Power of Speech, to every Limb;
" Tho' mask'd and mute, convey'd his quick
" Intent,
" And told in Frolic Gestures all he meant—
" But now the motly Coat, and Sword of Wood,
" Requires a Tongue to make them understood.

This particular Genius, so well described in the above Lines, engaged his Attention to Pantomimes, for which he had a true Taste, and that necessary Spirit for Expence, without which those Exhibitions cannot subsist; his Success therefore was owing to his own Personal Merit, because by that Assistance he withstood the greatest

Force of acting, and was able with an indifferent Company of Actors (sometimes the Refuse of the other Theatre) to leave at his Death a considerable Fortune to his Family.

N. B. The before mentioned very pompous Representation of the *Coronation*, brought several crouded Houses—After the run of that was over, appeared

January 1762.

THE LYAR, a Comedy of three Acts, by Mr. *Foote*.

This petit Comedy is taken from the *French*, as was Sir *Richard Steele*'s Lying Lovers. This new Piece was well received by the Public.

ARTAXERXES, an *English* Opera, translated from an *Italian* Opera of that

that Name: The Music composed by Dr. *Arne*, which was well performed in all its Parts. The Excellence of the Music of this Opera, has been confirmed by many crouded Audiences.

THE COUNTERFEIT, a Farce. Author unknown.

N. B. At the Conclusion of acting Plays this Season at *Drury-Lane* Theatre, which ended the 3d of *June* 1762—the Managers agreed with Mr. *Foote* and another Gentleman, for that Theatre for the Performance of a Summer Company, under their Management, and they exhibited the following new Pieces.

ALL IN THE WRONG, a *Comedy*, taken from the Cocu Imaginaire of *Molliere*, by Mr. *Murphy*.

This Comedy was excellently well acted in all its Parts, and received with great Applause.

THE CITIZEN, a Comedy of three Acts, and

THE OLD MAID, of two Acts.

Both by Mr. *Murphy*, and performed on the same Night. These two Pieces were well received by the Audience; particularly the *Old Maid*, which was performed very deservedly with universal Applause.

THE WISHES, founded on the *Italian* Comedy.

This Comedy had the good Fortune to captivate a certain Nobleman lately deceased, who engaged all the Nobility then in *London* in its Interest; but no

Power

Power can support a Play that is without Dramatic Merit, on the *English Stage*. The Hero of this Piece is *Harlequin!* he was the Lover and fine Gentleman; by his usual Magical Powers he had every thing he *wished for*— but in the last Scene being on a Couch toying with his Mistress, he wantonly (but unluckily) *wished he might be hanged,* when a Gibbet instantly rose from behind the Couch, which drew him up by the Neck into the Air, where he hung, dangling, a very wretched, dismal Spectacle! The Audience, who had shewn some Disapprobation before, took this Opportunity to join in the Execution.—It must however

however be observed, that in many Scenes of this Comedy, there are some very proper satirical Strokes on the false Taste and Fashion of the Times.

But this Article must not pass without the following Anecdote: While this Comedy was in Rehearsal, a printed Letter appeared directed to the Author *R. B.* Esq. setting forth, that it had been rejected by Mr. *Garrick*, in the following Words.—" But
" that any one who professes
" himself a Man of Taste, a
" Lover of the Belles Lettres, a
" Sovereign Critic in Dramatic
" Performances, and one who
" is himself a Dabler in the
" Business, should so far forget
" himself,

"himself, as to *reject a Work of* "*so much Wit and Ingenuity,* "*and such inimitable Raillery;*" (again)—" I received such a "Confirmation of my Judgment "by the Reception it met with "from the most celebrated Wits "of the Age—— It would be "ridiculous to suppose you any "longer regret the Reception it "met with at the Theatre"— meaning the Rejection by the above named Manager. Now the real Truth of the Story stands thus —The late Mr. *D*—— had been very justly distinguished in his Days of Manhood for his Taste in the Belles Lettres— but just at this Time, being created Lord *M*——— at the Verge

Verge of *Fourscore*,—this Comedy was put into his Hands for his Patronage, which touching the old Cause, and striking hard on the String of Vanity, his Lordship teazed and folicited all the Men of Quality he could come at to affift him to fupport this Work of Merit.—Many Lords did attend the firft Night's Performance; the Reception the three firft Acts met with was favourable, but towards the Conclufion, a general Difapprobation arofe which continued to the End: And what was the Confequence? A very thin Audience came to the fecond Performance—and to the third (the Author's Night) a much worfe
—under

—under Charges! Thus fell this great Phænomenon, about which such Wonders were related, and our Expectations so highly raised.

DRURY-LANE THEATRE.

September 1762.

THE WITCHES, a new Pantomime, compofed by Mr. *Love*, performed with Succefs.

THE TWO GENTLEMEN of VERONA, a *Comedy*, written by *Shakefpear*, revifed with Alterations and Additions by Mr. *Victor*.

When this Comedy was advertized to be printed by Mr. *Tonfon*, with the Alterations and Additions, the Public were promifed a Preface, containing critical Remarks on the numerous Editors of *Shakefpear*'s Works; but, for fome private Reafons, that Preface was suppressed; and the following Advertisement alone was printed before the Play.

Advertisement.

"IT is the general Opinion that this Co-
"medy abounds with Weeds; and there
"is no one, I think, will deny who pe-
"ruses it with Attention, that it is adorned
"with several poetical Flowers, such as
"the Hand of *Shakespear* alone could raise.
"The rankest of those Weeds I have en-
"deavoured to remove; but was not a
"little solicitous lest I should go too far,
"and, while I fancied myself grubbing up
"a Weed, should heedlessly cut the Threads
"of a Flower. The other Part of my
"Design, which was to give a greater
"Uniformity to the Scenery, and a Con-
"nection and Consistency to the Fable
                                    "(which

" (which in many Places is vifibly wanted)
" will be deemed of more Importance, if
" it fhould be found to be executed with
" Succefs.

" As to the two additional Scenes of
" *Launce* and *Speed* in the laft Act, I fhall
" leave them to the candid Judges of Dra-
" matic Compofition, whether they con-
" tribute any thing to the Reprefentation,
" or afford any Amufement to the Reader."

I cannot find upon the ftricteft Enquiry, this Comedy was ever acted fince the Time of its immortal Author; it is, undoubtedly, one of the moft weak and irregular of his Plays; which, I fuppofe, occafioned the following fevere Sentence from one of *Shakefpear's* numerous Editors—" *That the*
" Two Gentlemen of Verona
" *was*

" *was not written by him*; but
" *after his Death, foisted in by*
" *the Bookfellers to swell the*
" *Volume.*"

It is clear that none of the Folio Editions of *Shakespear*'s Plays were printed during his Life; and so careless were the Persons who had the Direction of the Press, that they printed the Prompter's Notes in the Margin (where Tables and Chairs are quoted) to direct the Stage-Keepers to be in Readiness against the changing the Scenes. Such gross Errors, and the Liberties taken by the Actors of altering Passages, agreeable to their Conceptions, called aloud for an Editor of Taste and Judgment!

Judgment! but then that chofen one ought to have been bleffed with a true Knowledge of his Author's *Genius* and *Stile*; had he been fo qualified, he muft have feen fuch evident Marks in many Scenes in the Comedy in queftion, to have convinced him it was the genuine Hand of that great Mafter.

I was greatly obliged to Mr. *Garrick*'s Friendfhip to employ me in this arduous undertaking, as his fole Motive was to do me Service; I had the Happinefs to fucceed fo far as to obtain his Approbation, and the fame Favour from the Public; but I was forry to find after I had furmounted the Difficulties I met

met with in the Scenery, and had happily introduced *Launce* and *Speed* in the laſt Act, that the *Fable* appears rather too weak to claim the due Attention of an improved Audience. That was not in my Power to amend.

It was performed five Nights with Succeſs; but on the ſixth (which according to Theatrical Cuſtom belongs to the Author of the Alterations) a very extraordinary Event happened. A Sett of young Men, who called themſelves the *Town*, had conſulted together, and determined to compel the Managers to admit them, at the End of the third Act, at half Price to every Performance, except *in the Run of a new Pantomime!* and they chose to make that Demand on the sixth Night of the *Two Gentlemen of Verona*, though it was printed on the Day-Bills, *for the Benefit of the Author of the Alterations.* It appeared afterwards a Rumour prevailed that Mr. *Garrick* was the Author; for, it must be supposed, they were ignorant of the Outrages they were committing on private Property; however, the Performance of the Play was actually forbid, and the Money (after the amount taken at the several Offices) returned to the Audience:—My Redress was undoubtedly to be obtained either from the Leader of this Troop

Troop (who was well known) or the Managers; but as the Rioters did much greater Damage to Covent-Garden Theatre, on the same Occasion, and as those in the Direction there, chose to give up all manner of Redress; the Managers of *Drury-Lane* were too wise to stand a Prosecution alone, therefore they followed the bad Example; and were so honourable to pay me one hundred Pounds, which was about the clear Sum, above the Charge of the House, on that sixth Night.

SPRING, a Pastoral, the Music by Mr. *Handell* and other eminent Masters.—It was well performed, and approved by the few who were Judges, and lovers of Music:—But these elegant Performances appear too languid after a Play, for the Galleries. Mr. *Norris*, now an excellent Tenor in the Oratorios, made his first Appearance in the above Pastoral.

THE MAGICIAN OF THE MOUNTAIN, a new Pantomime, by *Guerini*, from *Italy*, who performed the Pantaloon, disliked the first Night. It seems, the silly Tricks that divert an *Italian* are too low and trifling, to please even an *Englishman* disposed to favour the Harlequinade.

January 1763.

ELVIRA, a Tragedy, by Mr. *Mallet*, taken from the famous *Ines de Castro*.

Caſtro. The Story of this Tragedy was originally taken from a Play in the *Spaniſh* Language. This Tragedy was performed ſeveral Nights with Succeſs, Mrs. *Cibber,* and Mr. *Garrick,* acting the principal Characters.

THE DISCOVERY, a Comedy, by Mrs. *Sheridan,* performed ſeventeen Nights with great Applauſe. Mr. *Sheridan* (though not engaged this Seaſon at any Theatre) acted the Part of Lord *Medway* in his Wife's Comedy, for which the Managers gave him the Sixteenth Night for his own Benefit: Mrs. *Sheridan* had the Merit of inventing her own Fable, and introducing two new Characters, —*Sir Harry and Lady Flutter,* two young married People both under Age, and both ridiculously unhappy: *Sir Anthony Branville* was a Character entirely new to Mr. *Garrick*; as in his other comic Characters he is remarkable for his great Ease, Spirit, and Expression, in this he seem'd utterly to have extinguish'd his natural Talents, and assum'd a dry, stiff, Manner, with an immoveable Face, and thus extracted from this pedantic Object (who assum'd every Passion without shewing a Spark of any in his Action or Features) much Entertainment for the Audience, and great Credit for the Author, and Actor.

COVENT-GARDEN THEATRE.

LOVE in a VILLAGE, a Ballad Opera, by Mr. *Bickerstaff*.

The Tunes in this Opera were chosen and adapted by Doctor *Arne*, and the favourite Singer, Miss *Brent*, appeared in it to great Advantage—All the other Characters were well perform'd. —On which Account it was acted as many Nights as the celebrated Beggar's Opera when it first appeared, and with as general Applause. This Piece is taken from the *Village Opera*, by Mr. *Charles Johnson*, acted at

Drury-

Drury-Lane Theatre in 1728—but greatly improved by Mr. *Bickerstaff*.

THE BOARDING SCHOOL, a Farce, Author unknown.

MARPLOT IN LISBON, a Farce, Do.

DRURY-LANE THEATRE.

THE 15th of *September* 1763, the Day of opening the Theatre Royal in *Drury-Lane*, Mr. *Garrick*, by the Advice of his Phyſician, left *London* to take the Tour of *Italy*; leaving his Brother, Mr. *George Garrick* as his Agent, to aſſiſt the premier Patentee, *James Lacy*, Eſq. in the Management; and Mr. *Powell* (who had his Inſtructions the Summer before) with Mr. *Holland*, to act the principal Characters, 'till his Return, which was in the Month of *April* 1765.

Nov. 1763.

PHILASTER, reviv'd, a Play of *Beaumont* and *Fletcher*'s; and eſteem'd the best of their serious Productions.—This Play was alter'd, and adapted to the present, improv'd, Stage, by *George Colman*, Esq; for the Introduction of Mr. *Powell* in the Character of *Philaster*, a young Adventurer—and the Play, but particularly the Actor, met with universal Applause.

LOVE AT FIRST SIGHT, a Farce of two Acts, by Mr. *King* Comedian, acted with Success.

THE DEUCE IS IN HIM, a Farce of two Acts, by *George Colman*, Esq. an excellent petite Piece: The Hint of Colonel *Tamper's* Suspicion, and the Trial of his Mistresse's Constancy, by his pretended Loss of an Eye and Leg,

[55]

Leg, is taken from one of the Tales of *Marmontel*, and well improv'd by Mr. *Colman* :—This Farce was perform'd several Nights with great Applause.

January 1764.

THE DUPE, a Comedy.

Though I delivered my Opinion of this Comedy, to my Friend the Authoress in its Disfavour, before it went to the Stage; yet the Fate it met with there surpriz'd me! I expected it to be, in general, disliked, but not treated with Ill-nature, as it was known to be the Work of a Lady, whose former Comedy and other Productions had been well receiv'd by the Public. The Groupe of Characters (and whole.

whole Busines of this Comedy) are of a disagreeable Cast; there is, however, some Merit in the bold Attempt at drawing a new Character, and of inventing her own Fable; which few of our modern Authors dare trust to, but shamefully fly to the *French* for Assistance.—There was one Critic (I think one of the Reviewers) that politely conveyed his Criticism in the following Words. " Mrs. *Sheridan* has " only fail'd in the drawing of " such Characters, which, as a " Woman of Reputation, she " could not be acquainted with."

1764.

THE RITES OF HECATE, OR HARLEQUIN FROM THE MOON, a Pantomime, by Mr. *Love.*

This Entertainment was like most of those Exhibitions; but as it was followed, and added to the Receipts of the Houses, every End was answered, and all Parties concerned satisfied.

THE ROYAL SHEPHERD, an *English* Opera, composed by Mr. *Rush*.

Mr. *Rush* was admitted, by the Judges of Music, to have done his Duty, and shewed himself a Master of Composition. This Opera was well received, but neglected.

N. B. This Opera was the last of the Novelties of this Season; which proved a very successful one,

DRURY-LANE THEATRE.

2d *November* 1764.

ALMENA, a serious Opera, written by Mr. *Rolt*, and set to Music by Mr. *Michael Arne*, and Mr. *Battishall*.—This Opera, though it met with a favourable Reception, was performed but six Nights, to thin Audiences.

28th.

CAPRICIOUS LOVERS, a comic Opera, written by the late Mr. *Robert Lloyd*, and set to Music by Mr. *Rush*.—The Plot was taken from the *French*, most of the Songs were

were well written, but the Fable in the laſt Act, too much neglected. This Opera was perform'd nine Nights, and the Muſic, in general, well approv'd.

24th *January* 1765.

THE PLATONIC WIFE, a Comedy. This Piece was written by Mrs. *Griffith*, a Lady well known and admired in the literary World, on Account of the Part ſhe bore in the ingenious Correſpondence between *Henry* and *Frances,* in two Volumes, which had been publiſh'd ſome Time before the acting this Play.

The Account ſhe gives of her Comedy, in her Preface, is in the following Words.

" The Hint of this Piece was taken from " one of the *Contes Moraux* of *Marmontel,* " ſtiled

" stil'd *L'Heureux Divorce*, the Foible ridi-
" culed in the Tale is, perhaps, the only
" one imputed to our Sex, which has never
" yet been expofed by a theatrical Repre-
" fentation; it is a Simplicity, not a Co-
" quetry—it is the Error of a delicate and
" elevated Mind, unacquainted with the
" Manners of real Life, or the general
" Frame of the human Heart.

" The Novel was too barren of Incident
" to furnifh out an Entertainment for the
" Stage; which obliged me to contrive an
" entire Under-plot, and introduce feveral
" new Characters into the Comedy, which
" I fhall not take up the Reader's Time to
" point out here, but fubmit this Perform-
" ance to the Candor and Clemency of the
" Public, after having, perhaps, too ad-
" venturoufly hazarded their Criticifm and
" Cenfure."

This Comedy was too severely treated by the Audience the first Night of its Representation, owing to the following Circumstances and Accidents.——The Character of the *Heroine*, and the Title of the Play did not perfectly agree—she was not a *Platonic* but a *Romantic* Wife, who had taken a Disgust at her Husband for having abated of the Attention, and Gallantries of the Lover after Marriage! The low Characters introduced into the Drama, was a forced Stile of Writing in the Author, who appears to have been wholly unacquainted with vulgar Life.

But the principal Misfortune was occasioned by the Accident

of

of two Portraits, upon which the interesting Part of the Fable was to turn; having been got up rather in too much Haste, they failed of their intended Effect; however, every Objection that had been hinted at by the Audience was obviated, as far as possible, against the second Representation; and as the Comedy is not without Merit in the Stile, Sentiment, and Moral, it received the Approbation of five successive Audiences.

THE TUTOR, a Farce of two Acts, the Author unknown. This Performance was treated as it deserved: the first Night's Audience gave it strong Marks of Disfavour—but the second seem'd to to repeat it with such Violence, that nothing but a Promise from the Stage, that it should be acted no more after that Night, could procure it a Hearing.

PHARNACES, a serious Opera, written by Mr. *Hull*, and set to Music by Mr. *Bates*; well receiv'd, but neglected——and perform'd six Nights to thin Audiences.

I will venture to make this Observation upon serious Operas—that notwithstanding the great Success some have met with, and the Encouragement given by People of Fashion to that exotic Entertainment (whether exhibited in *Italian* or *English*) they are not, or ever can be adapted to the *English* Taste, in general.

THE CHOICE, a Farce of two Acts,—got up for the Benefit of Mrs. *Yates*.

Yates. This little Comedy (for it could with no Degree of Propriety be call'd a Farce) was well acted, and well receiv'd; and as it has never since appear'd, either on the Stage, or in Print, it was supposed to be sent forth, at that Time, to serve Mrs. *Yates,* and try its Worth.

COVENT-GARDEN THEATRE

APPEARS to be, at this Juncture, the Seat of Mufic and *Englifh* Operas:—under the Management of the late Mr. *Rich*, it was juftly diftinguifhed for *Pantomimes*—and now, under the Direction of his Son-in-Law, Mr. *Beard*, *Mufic* muft have its Reign, and be properly fupported by the beft *Englifh* Singers;—the firft new mufical Performance this Year was,

Nov. 1764.

THE GUARDIAN OUTWITTED, a Comedy of five Acts, interfperfed with Songs for all the Characters.

Doctor

Doctor Arne, (who is undoubtedly one of our first Geniuses in Music) was the Composer of the Songs, but denies being the Author of this strange, medley Performance: His appearing the first Night at the Harpsicord, to attend his Music, as usual, brought this Disgrace upon him, and the Minor Critics, upon this Information alone, abused him unmercifully in Epistles, Epigrams, Songs, and Pamphlets.

NO ONE's ENEMY BUT HIS OWN, a Comedy of three Acts, and, WHAT WE MUST ALL COME TO, a Comedy of two Acts;—it was said, that Party interfered to condemn these two Pieces very undeservedly.

MIDAS, a Burlesque Opera.——This Opera was written, and the Music fic for the Songs chosen and adapted by Mr. *O'Hara*, a Gentleman of *Ireland*, of great Taste and Knowledge in Music:—It was first performed at the Theatre Royal in *Dublin*, with Applause; which has been confirmed by the Audiences of *London*.

ABSENT MAN, a Farce, by Mr. *Bickerstaff*. This little Piece met with a favourable Reception.

SHEPHERD's ARTIFICE, a Pastoral.

ALEXANDER THE LITTLE, a Farce. Very little known.

SPANISH LADY, a Ballad Farce. This little Piece was written by Mr. *Hull*, and perform'd on his own Benefit Night—and (as a

Proof

Proof it has Merit) several Times since with Success.

SUMMER's TALE, a Comedy of three Acts.—The Story, or Fable of this little Comedy is pleasing, and the Songs well written; which was the general Opinion of the Audience, who gave it a favourable Reception :——And surely the Author's modest Motto, *Vox et præterea nihil*—must disarm the critical Reader from exercising his Severity in the Closet.

THE MAID OF THE MILL, a Dramatic Opera, by Mr. *Bickerstaff*.—This Gentleman chose and adapted the Music to his Songs, and chiefly from *Italian* Burlettas.—The Parts were all extremely

tremely well perform'd, and prov'd an agreeable Entertainment:—It was receiv'd by the Audience with univerſal Applauſe, and had a Run of Thirty-five Nights to crowded Houſes.

DRURY-LANE THEATRE.

8th *October* 1765.

DAPHNE AND AMINTOR, a Dramatic Paftoral.—This was the *Oracle*, brought on the Stage by Mrs. *Cibber*, about fifteen Years ago, and tranflated by her from the *French*.—As fhe performed this little elegant Piece, it was acted feveral Times at both Theatres, and at the Theatre Royal in *Dublin*, with great Succefs. Mr. *Bickerftaff* faw it lately on the *French* Stage at *Paris*, and was charm'd with it there:—Says in his Preface, that he he has tranflated and enriched it with feveral Songs for all the Characters, adapted to *Italian* Mufic—and by the happy Figure and excellent Performance of Mifs *Wright* (now Mrs. *Arne*) this Piece was exhibited Twenty-three Nights with great Succefs.

7th *December.*

THE PLAIN DEALER, a Comedy alter'd from *Wycherly*—by Mr. *Bickerftaff.*—The *Plain Dealer* of *Wycherly* was efteem'd the *Chef d'œuvre* of all his Works, and a conftant Stock Play 'till thefe laft Thirty Years:—But, to the Honour of the prefent Age, no fuch grofs Scenes as are in the Old Play will be endured:—Mr. *Bickerftaff* has not only made this Comedy

Comedy decent, but entertaining :—Yet the feverer Critics fay (but unjuftly) it is like reforming an old Libertine, and leaving him dull and infipid ;—yet, furely, it is a public Benefit to correct the Vices of an *agreeable* Libertine, though the Operation in fome Meafure might lower his Spirits.

6th *Jan.* 1766.

THE HERMIT, OR HARLEQUIN AT RHODES, a new Pantomime—compofed by Mr. *Love*, &c. This Exhibition was much followed, and brought feveral crowded Houfes, and the Succefs chiefly owing to the Reports our News-papers were, at that Time, daily filled with, of the *French* wild

wild Beaſt, that was devouring (and yet purſued by) Children. —This wild Beaſt was happily introduced in this Pantomime, purſued by Boys, led on by a *Frenchman.*—At laſt the Beaſt made his Re-entry, and ran across the Stage with the poor *Frenchman* in his Mouth, to the great Joy of the Pit, Box, and Galleries.

20th *Feb.*

THE CLANDESTINE MARRIAGE, a Comedy, by *George Colman*, and *David Garrick*, Eſqrs; performed with great Applauſe, and continues to this Day a favourite Comedy.—What leſs can be expected from the Dramatic partnerſhip of two ſuch Geniuſes?—

The Part of *Lord Ogleby* was plan'd and written by Mr. *Garrick*, and intended to be perform'd by himself:———But after his Travels into *Italy* for his Health, and his Return after two Years to the Stage, having determined to perform in no New Play, becaufe the Run might be attended with Fatigue and Inconvenience to him—He very wifely gave up this capital Part to Mr. KING—a Comedian of rifing Merit; who, by his excellent Performance of *Lord Ogleby*, eftablifhed his *Reputation*.

FALSTAFF's WEDDING, a Comedy, by Mr. *Kenrick*,—brought on the Stage by Mr. *Love*, on his own Benefit Night, and well received

received by the Audience.—The Critics allowed the Character of *Sir John Falstaff* was well imitated; and the Stile and Manner of *Shakespeare*, better supported in several Scenes, than by any Author that has made the same Attempt.

THE HOBBY HORSE, a Farce of two Acts.—This Hobby Horse, not proving the Hobby Horse of the Audience, it was acted that Night only.

COVENT-GARDEN THEATRE.

Feb. 1766.

THE DOUBLE MISTAKE, a Comedy, by Mrs. *Griffith.*

This Play met with a reversed Fate of her *Platonic Wife:* Her private Friends advised her very prudently to conceal herself. And though it was favourably received by those who presided at that Theatre as Managers, the Actors who were cast into the Parts, gave it an unfavourable Report, a Fault they ought never to commit; however, the first

first Night's Audience differed with them in Opinion, and gave it great Applause! The Story is pleasing, and the Expectation, by two or three lucky Incidents, kept up to the Catastrophe:—It was performed Twelve Nights, with general Approbation.

THE ACCOMPLISHED MAID.

This musical Performance is a Translation of the celebrated *Burletta*, performed with great Success at the Opera House called *la Buona Figliuola*—which this Translator has transformed into the *Accomplished Maid*, but this Alteration in Title and Stile of Music, &c. soon procured a colder Reception from the Public

lic in *Covent-Garden*, than the *Good Girl* met with in the *Hay-Market*.

THE SCHOOL FOR GUARDIANS, a Comedy.

This Comedy is taken from two *French* Plays, by a Gentleman who has written several successful Pieces:——But this Performance met with a cool Reception.

THE PERPLEXITIES, a Comedy, and FAIRY FAVOUR, both by Mr. *Hull*.

The Fairy Favour is a little musical Pastoral, taken from *Shakespeare*'s Fairies, and intended as a Compliment to the young *Prince of Wales*, at his first going to *Covent-Garden* Theatre.

LOVE IN THE CITY, a Dramatic Opera.

This Performance met with an unfavourable Reception. The Audience expected better Entertainment from the Author of the *Maid of the Mill*.

N. B. The Entrance of this Year 1766, was made remarkable by the Death of two illustrious Personages in the Drama, Mrs. *Cibber*, and Mr. *Quin*. —On the 30th of *January*, Mrs. *Cibber* departed this Life. She was born in the Year 1715.

Every Age, or Half Century, has their favourite, celebrated Actor, or Actress: Mrs. *Cibber* very justly enjoyed that Happiness for more than twenty Years; the first Part this Actress appeared in was *Zara*, then translated from *Voltaire*, by

Aaron

Aaron Hill, Efq; in the Year 1734—and at her firſt Appearance became a favourite with the Public.

As I had been very early acquainted with the Families of the *Arnes* and the *Cibbers*—I knew her Marriage with Mr. *Theophilus Cibber* was very much againſt her Inclination; and the Misfortunes that attended it (of which the Public were at the Time fully informed) interrupted her Progreſs in the Buſineſs of the Stage for many Years: But for the laſt Twenty, ſhe remained in the quiet Poſſeſſion of all the capital Characters, and in the Hearts of the enamoured Public! Her Voice was muſically plaintive—in Parts of Softneſs and Diſtreſs, ſhe appeared truly amiable—without being remarkable for *Beauty*, *Gentility*, or *Elegance of Dreſs*.

In

In the *School for Lovers*, she performed the Part of *Cælia*, whose Age is mentioned in the Play to be Sixteen—and Mrs. *Cibber* was admitted to become the Character by the nicest Observers, though she was at that Time, approaching to Fifty! This strange, seeming Absurdity, was entirely owing to that uncommon Symmetry, and exact Proportion in her Form, that happily remained with her to her Death.

About a Month before she died, the Comedy of the *Provok'd Wife* was commanded by their *Majesties*, to see Mr. *Garrick* in *Sir John Brute* after his Return from *Italy*, where he had been two Years. Mrs. *Cibber* appeared in the Part of *Lady Brute*. This was her last, and, I am sorry to say, her worst Performance.

Of all the Variety and Extent of the Tragic Passions, I know of none equal to that

that of *Conſtance* in *King John*; Mrs. *Cibber* ſurpaſſed all that have followed her in that Character.—When ſhe enter'd with diſſhevel'd hair, and Wildneſs in her Eyes! having loſt her Son—" *her pretty Arthur!*" The Cardinal, and others attempting to comfort her—ſhe ſunk on the Ground—and looking round with a dignified Wildneſs and Horror! ſaid,

" Here *I*, and *Sorrow* ſit!—this is my *Throne!*—
" Let *Kings* come bow to it—!"

Nothing that ever was exhibited, could exceed this Picture of Diſtreſs! And nothing that ever came from the Mouth of Mortal was ever ſpoken with more dignified Propriety!——The late Mrs. *Wiffington*, who was excellent in many Parts of this Character, could never ſucceed in this particular Paſſage.—Mrs. *Cibber* never executed it without a Burſt of Applauſe

from

from the whole Audience! With Mrs. *Woffington* it was lefs noticed than many other Parts of that Character—and though I had the Pleafure of being very intimate with that agreeable Actrefs, and often mentioned this Circumftance to her, and have been often with her, when fhe has tried to execute what I have defcribed, yet on the Stage it ever failed.

I have endeavoured to give a very faint Idea of Mrs. *Cibber*'s Excellence in *Conftance!* But who can be capable of conveying to thofe who have not had the delightful Satisfaction of feeing her, the peculiar Looks of Diftrefs! and the Powers of her Action, when fhe was fully animated with her Character? The *Painter*'s Art lives on the Canvas—but the *Actor*'s muft die with him! This Truth is feelingly convey'd in the following Lines, which were introduced in the Prologue, written by Mr. *Garrick*, to the Comedy of the *Clandestine Marriage*, which, at the same Time, bears the best Testimony to the Merits of his Contemporaries, Mr. *Quin* and Mrs. *Cibber*——

The *Painter* † dead, yet still he charms the Eye;
While *England* lives, his Fame can never die:
But He, who struts his Hour upon the Stage,
Can scarce extend his Fame to half an Age;
Nor Pen, nor Pencil, can the Actor save,
The Art, and Artist, share one common Grave.
   O let me drop, one tributary Tear,
On poor JACK FALSTAFF's Grave, and JULIET's
      Bier!
You, to their Worth, must Testimony give;
'Tis in your Hearts alone their Fame can live.
Still as the Scenes of Life will shift away,
The strong Impressions of their Art decay:

---

† HOGARTH—whose excellent Paintings of *Marriage à la-Mode*, gave the Hint to the Authors of the *Clandestine Marriage*.

Your Children cannot feel what you have known;
They'll boaſt of *Quins* and *Cibbers* of their own.
The greateſt Glory of our happy Few,
Is to be felt, and be approv'd by *You*.

Mrs. *Cibber* was privately buried in *Weſtminſter Abbey*, and her Pall ſupported by Perſons of great Diſtinction.

In the *March* following died at *Bath* (to which Place he had wiſely retired for many Years,) the CELEBRATED Mr. JAMES QUIN, in the Seventy-third Year of his Age. If the complete Performance of one ſingle Part in the long Liſt of the Drama, can give an Actor a juſt Title to that Epithet, he enjoyed it with great Truth, for he was *inimitable* in the Character of *Falſtaff*.

After Mr. *Booth* left the Stage in the Year 1728, Mr. *Quin* became the principal Actor in Tragedy; and a few Years bringing a new Set of Auditors to the Theatre, who never faw a better, he was foon eftablifhed the moft eminent of his Profeffion:—But I muft here obferve, though I have only mentioned his FALSTAFF as INIMITABLE, that he had great Merit in the *Spanifh Fryer—Comus—*the *Duke in Meafure for Meafure—Æfop,* and fome other Parts of that Caft. Thus he remained 'till the Appearance of Mr. *Garrick!* When that Star fhone forth in the Theatrical Hemifphere, Mr. *Quin*'s Luftre, as a Tragedian, foon began to diminifh; and his Manner to be called *antiquated—*though he was not above the Age of Fifty! And thus by him the *Old Stile* of Acting (as the Phrafe is) came into Difrepute.

Mr. *Quin,* who was famous for *Bons Mots—*when he found Mr. *Garrick* was followed, and brought crouded Houfes, faid, That *Garrick was a new Religion;* Whitfield

field was followed for a Time, but they would all come to *Church* again.

Mr. *Garrick* gave him the Retort courteous, in the following Reply:

" *Pope-Quin*, who damns all Churches but his own,
" Complains that *Heresy*, corrupts the Town;
" That *Whitfield-Garrick* has misled the Age,
" And taints the found Religion of the Stage;
" Schism, he cries, has turn'd the Nation's Brain,
" But, Eyes will open, and to *Church* again!"
Thou great Infallible!—forbear to roar,
Thy Bulls, and Errors, are rever'd no more;
When Doctrines meet with general Approbation,
It is not *Heresy*, but *Reformation*.

I was seldom absent from Mr. *Quin*'s principal Performances in the prime Part of his Life—from Thirty to Forty.—At that Age whatever Genius the Actor is bless'd with, must be fully brought forth. —He was then at the Head of the *Lincoln's Inn Fields* Company, where he generally per-

perform'd his principal Characters to indifferent Houses.—And indeed when he appeared in the same Parts that were then acted at *Drury-Lane* Theatre, by Mr. *Booth*, it ceased to be a Wonder! Now, if Mr. *Quin* stood thus with the Town when in his prime of Life, I shall leave my Reader to judge how capable he was in his Decline, of conveying a Sample of any *old Manner* of Acting, but his own! If Mr. *Booth* was unable to describe Mr. *Betterton*'s Excellence (as I have heard him say) I am sure Mr. *Quin* was in no Degree able to give the least Shadow of Mr. *Booth*'s!

Some of Mr. *Quin*'s Friends with whom he sometimes corresponded, have assured me, he was deficient in Literature, and laugh'd at those who read Books, by way of Enquiry after Knowledge, saying, He read

Men

Men—that the *World* was the best Book. —If this was true, what an amazing Strength of natural Parts must he have been bless'd with, to be able to make the Figure he did as a Man of Sense and Genius!

From the Death of Mr. *Booth*, in the Year 1733, to the powerful Appearance of Mr. *Garrick* (a Period of ten or twelve Years) Mr. *Quin* was the first in the Profession, and then began to make his Fortune; I am well informed his Power was so great as to demand 800 Pounds a-Year Salary; which Mr. *Rich* was then obliged to comply with! No wonder that at such a fortunate Juncture, he collected a Sum sufficient to enable him to retire to the full Enjoyment of all the Comforts and Blessings of this Life, for which no Man had an higher Relish. He was an

excellent

excellent Companion, when kept within proper Bounds—and died with the Character of a sensible, witty, honest Man.

Though it is foreign to the Design of this Work to have any Thing to do with Biography, yet I am tempted to introduce the following very remarkable Anecdote, relating to this great Actor, which has been lately sent me, attested by two worthy Gentlemen, to whom Mr. *Quin* related it some Time before his Death.

His Mother was a reputed Widow, w͞ had been married to a Person in the mer̄cantile Way, and who left her in *Ireland* to pursue some Traffick, or particular Business in the *West Indies*.—He had been absent from her near seven Years, without having received any Letter, or the least Information about him. He was given out to be dead, which Report was univer-

sally

fally credited; she went into Mourning for him; and some Time after a Gentleman whose Name was *Quin*, who had an Estate of a Thousand Pounds a-Year, paid his Addresses to her, and married her.—She bore him a Son—and no Couple appeared more happy—but in the midst of their Happiness—the first Husband returned—claim'd his Wife—and had her. Mr. *Quin* retired with his Son—and at his Death left him his Estate:—But the Heir at Law, hearing the Story of our Hero—soon recovered the Estate, and left young *Quin* to shift for himself, in what Manner his Wit and Genius would suggest to him; —he soon took to the Stage, where he got both *Fame* and *Fortune*; and counterbalanc'd by his Talents, the untoward Accidents of his Birth.

Before I quit this Subject, I must insert
in

in this Place, that excellent Epigram of Mr. *Garrick*'s, written about a Year before Mr. *Quin* died; which, as a true Lover of Wit and Humor, no one admired more than himself.

A Soliloquy by Mr. *Quin*, upon seeing the Body of *Duke Humphry*, at the Cathedral of *St. Albans*.

A Plague of *Egypt*'s Arts I say;
Embalm the Dead! on senseless Clay,
 Rich Wines and Spices waste;
Like Sturgeon, or like Brawn, shall I
Bound in a precious Pickle lie,
 Which I can never taste?

(II.)

Let me embalm this Flesh of mine,
With Turtle fat, and *Bourdeaux* Wine,
 And spoil the *Egyptian* Trade!
Than good Duke *Humphry*, happier I,
Embalm'd alive; *Old Quin* shall die,
 A *Mummy* ready made!

As

As a Proof that we cannot part with those with whom we have spent most of our joyous Hours without a Sigh—the following Lines appear'd soon after the Death of Mr. *Quin*, from the same eminent Hand, and are engrav'd upon his Monument, in the Abbey Church of *Bath*.

Epitaph.

That Tongue, which *set the Table on a Roar !*
And charm'd the publick Ear, is heard no more;
Clos'd are those Eyes, the Harbingers of Wit,
Which spake before the Tongue, what *Shakespear* writ;
Cold is that Hand, which living was stretch'd forth,
At Friendship's Call, to succour modest Worth;
Here lies *James Quin*—deign Reader, to be taught,
Whate'er thy Strength of Body, Force of Thought,
In Nature's happiest Mould, however cast,
" To this Complexion Thou must come at last."

I hope the Reader will excuse me for dwelling thus long on the Characters of Persons so eminent in their Profession; and who, when living, were so great an Ornament to the Stage.

THEATRE ROYAL

DRURY-LANE.

25th Oct. 1766.

THE COUNTRY GIRL, a Comedy—almoſt new written by Mr. *Garrick*, on the Plan of the *Country Wife*, by Wycherly, and for the ſame Reaſon already aſſigned for altering his Plain Dealer; though I think in the *Country Wife* he was ſtill a greater Offender; but it muſt be admitted that the Libertines in *Wycherly*'s Time were allowed greater Latitude than thoſe of our Days.——I believe there are few

few greater Alterations in *London*, than thofe which have been made in our Theatres: After the total Demolition of Plays, and Actors, in the Reign of *Fanaticifm*, and the happy Reftoration, to Monarchy and Pleafures, it was no Wonder they changed from the hateful Mode of *Oliver*'s Days, into a contrary Extream.—Their Theatres were much fmaller than ours, and proportion'd to their Audiences, which feldom exceeded feventy Pounds;—very few went thither but the young and gay of both Sexes, and the *Ladies in Mafks*, which feemed to be a tacit Confeffion that the Entertainment they expected to meet with was not of the moft modeft modest Kind.—This new written Comedy was well received by the Audience.

18th *Nov.*

NECK or NOTHING, partly from the *French*, a Farce of two Acts, Author unknown.

This Piece was performed seven or eight Nights with tolerable Succefs.—The Characters are truly Farcical, and were well performed—and yet as the Public have of late been so much entertained with intriguing Servants—this Farce did not meet with the Reception it deserved.

21st *Nov.*

THE CUNNING MAN, a musical Pastoral, from the *Devin de Village* of *Rousseau*, who also composed

posed the Music, to attempt at giving the *French* a better Taste by uniting *Sense* with *Sound*.— This Performance was acted seven or eight Nights, and met with a cold Reception:—But several *English* Gentlemen who saw it in the *French* Theatre, told me, It was with some Difficulty they could discover it to be the same Piece, that gave them so much Pleasure at *Paris*.

13th *Decemb*.

THE EARL of WARWICK, a Tragedy, imitated from the *French* of Monsieur *de le Harpe*.

The Reverend Gentleman who is the Author of this Play, has given several Instances of his Abilities as an Author; and in this

this Tragedy there are many spirited Scenes, and popular Strokes of Art, sufficient to support it—Most of the capital Characters were well performed—particularly *Margaret of Anjou* by Mrs. *Yates*, who did that Part, and consequently herself eminent Service.—I heard some of the graver Critics not a little disgusted with the Author, for chusing a noted historical Story and varying so much from the Fact:—It was indeed great Pity that he found himself obliged to alter the Conduct of his Hero in the last Act, so much to his Disadvantage.—However, this Tragedy was performed ten Nights, and very justly applauded.

2d Jan. 1767.

CYMON, a Dramatic Romance. The Author of *Cymon*, who has not thought proper to affix his Name to the printed Copy, is well known to be as happy in all his Theatrical Compositions, as in his personal Performances on the Stage; where he remains to this Day the Nonpareil.——— This Dramatic Romance gave great Scope to his fruitful Imagination, as every Thing within the Powers of Machinery are to be done by Magic.—The Scenes are extremely fine, some of them were designed by a Master brought from *Italy!* But the greatest Scene of all at the End, with its Preparation, was *English*

Invention, and *English* Execution:—The Connoisseurs and Critics in Music lamented, that, to the great Expence of Scenery, this Author had not added that of employing the best Composer for the Songs.—This Piece was well performed in all its Parts, and brought several crouded Audiences.

21st *Feb.*

THE ENGLISH MERCHANT, a Comedy, by *George Colman*, Esq.

This Gentleman has given manifest Proof of his Genius for Theatrical Writings.—This Play was performed several Nights with great Applause.—But many Admirers of Mr. *Colman* as a Dramatic Writer, were sorry he adhered

adhered so closely to *Voltaire*; and wished he had done more from himself, which would, undoubtedly, have been better for the Play, the Author, and the Public.

24th *March*.

MEDEA, a Tragedy, by *Richard Glover*, Esq.

This Tragedy was written near forty Years ago; about that Period I had the Pleasure of being introduced to the Acquaintance of the ingenious and worthy Author; and then among other of his poetical Pieces, enjoyed the *Medea*. In the Year 1732, I introduced the Author to the late Mr. *Booth* to read this Tragedy to him; who was very much

much charmed with the Sentiments and the poetical Part—but gave his Opinion, that it was an unfit Subject for an *English* Audience:—However Mrs. *Porter* was applied to, being the only Actress then living, that could appear in that capital Character.—But the Accident she met with of breaking her Thigh, by an Overturn in her Chaise, put an End to the Attempt:—The Author some few Years ago gave this Tragedy to the Press;—and Mrs. *Yates* was encouraged by some of her judicious Friends to get it up this Year for her Benefit Play: She acquitted herself in that difficult Character to Admiration:——

I know

I know several Gentlemen of Learning and Genius, that wish to have the *Medea* one Night annually performed, to shew how well an *English* Genius can imitate, and rival the ancient, *Greek* Tragedy.

DIDO, a Tragedy.

A manuscript Copy of this Tragedy was put into my Hands one Day at a Visit five or six Years ago, to my late noble Friend Lord *Southwell*, who made it his Request, that I would not only read it with Attention, but return it to his Lordship, with my Opinion in Writing. I did not like the Office, but found myself obliged to accept it. I soon returned the Copy with a short

short Letter, as desired, which I remember was to this Effect;—
"*That I thought the Author very unhappy in the Choice of his Fable—as every School-Boy was acquainted with the Fate of Dido and Æneas;—that there was Merit in the Stile and Sentiment, which would have served a better Subject.*"

Mr. *Holland*, some Time after, employed his Influence with the Managers, to consent to his getting up this Tragedy for his annual Benefit Play; —The Favour was great; and none but a capital Performer could ask it, or expect to succeed; the Play was well acted—Mrs. *Yates* and Mr. *Powell* were the

Dido

Dido and *Æneas.*—Mr. *Holland* (as the Profits of the Night were for himſelf) took a ſecond Character; and (as I have already obſerved) the Tragedy having ſome Merit, the Audience gave it a favourable Reception; it was performed once or twice, ſoon after, for the mutual Benefit of the Managers and the Author:—But the Seaſon was too far advanced for any ſucceſsful Conſequences.

N. B. The ingenious Author of this *Tragedy* and the *Regiſter Office*, being by Profeſſion a *Rope Maker*—I ſhall cloſe this Subject (and the Seaſon) with the following Witty Prologue, which was ſpoken by Mr. *King*, and received with very great Applauſe.

PROLOGUE to *DIDO*,
(Written by Mr. *Garrick.*)

A Rope Maker a Poet!—write a Play!
O—hang the Blockhead—wicked Wits will say;
——Before you turn him off—a Word I pray.
Genius is not to Place, or State fix'd down,
But flies at Random, all about the Town;
Now at *Whitehall*, now at *St. James*'s smiles;
Then whisks to *Wapping*, or to Broad *St. Giles:*
O let not Prejudice, rank Weed, take Root;
Which may of Genius, choak the fairest Fruit;
If none but Gentlemen high-born must write,
I fear we soon should wish you all good Night:
Shakespear, and *Johnson,* our Dramatic Lords,
Did they amuse themselves with twisting Cords?
Were they fine Gentlemen?——O—no—Old *Ben*
Was famous for his *Trowell,* and his *Pen;*
With Mortar, and the Muse, he pass'd his Days,
And built good Walls, before he built good Plays.
Shakespear, a Genius born!—his Taste was such,
Too exquisite! He lov'd fat Buck too much!
And he whose matchless Muse can soften Rocks,
Fled to Parnassus to avoid the Stocks.

Now

Now to the Rope Maker I come again——
Who having spun much Hemp, now spins his Brain;
This *Hempen* Produce any Test will stand;
This, of his Brain, may prove a Rope of Sand;
But should this Spinning of his Head deceive him,
This Hempen Manufacture may relieve him!
Had I but Time to give my Fancy scope,
I'd shew, how *Tragedy* was like a *Rope*,
How several Parts well twisted, make a Whole
To curb the Passions, and to melt the Soul.
The Cause of Justice each alike befriends,
Both salutary Means for moral Ends;
Thus the most crabbed *Critic* plainly sees,
That making *Ropes*, is writing *Tragedies*.
And should he fail to please—poor, scribbling Elf—
O—then he makes a Rope to hang himself.

DRURY-LANE THEATRE.

23d *October* 1767.

PEEP BEHIND THE CURTAIN, or NEW REHEARSAL, a Comedy of two Acts—performed several Nights with great Applause.—The ingenious Author had certainly done something more than *Peep* behind the Curtain, for Nobody seems to be better acquainted with the Humours that pass there than himself.

5th *Decem*.

THE WIDOW'D WIFE, a Comedy, by Mr. *Kenrick*,——performed fourteen

fourteen Nights, and well received.

THE ELOPEMENT. The machinery Part of this *Pantomime* was invented by Mr. *Maſſink* from the Theatre Royal in *Dublin*: Theſe Scenes were ſhowy, and well executed; and the comic Part conducted with more Humor than we generally ſee in thoſe Entertainments.

Jan. 6th 1768.

THE COUNTESS OF SALISBURY, a Tragedy, by *Hall Hartſtone,* Eſq. a Student of Trinity College *Dublin,*—and was acted ſeveral Nights at the Theatre Royal in that City with Applauſe.—When the Manager of that Theatre appeared the ſecond

Summer

Summer in Connection with Mr. *Foote* (who had then new-built his Theatre under a Royal Patent) he perform'd this Tragedy with repeated Succefs——Mr. *Barry* and Mrs. *Dancer* being engaged the following Seafon at *Drury-Lane* Theatre, they performed the *Countefs of Salifbury* there; but the more critical Winter-Audiences received it with lefs Warmth.

23d.
FALSE DELICACY, a Comedy, by Mr. *Hugh Kelly*.

This is another of the grave fentimental Plays called a Comedy, which is very properly, as well as humouroufly, banter'd in the Prologue—the Author (there

(there) calls it *supporting the Dignity of Writing, and the Chastity of the Stage*—which ought to be the Province and Duty of the Tragic Muse—but surely the Comic Lady should ridicule the *Foibles* of Mankind, and make us laugh at their pleasant Situations.—This Play was well performed, and received with universal Applause.—The Fable is interesting: The Character of *Cecil* is well drawn, and has an Air of Originality that does Credit to the Author; Mrs. *Harley* was well supported by Mrs. *Dancer*—and the happy Vein of Humour thrown into the Epilogue, was so well executed by this Actress—that even a weak
Play

Play would have been strengthened by it.

27th *Feb.*

ZENOBIA, a Tragedy, by *Arthur Murphy*, Esq.

This Tragedy had very great Success, and is allow'd to have many true Dramatic Requisites; the Story is in *Tacitus*, and the celebrated *Crebillon* has wrote a *French* Tragedy on this Subject, of which our Author owns in his Prologue, he has availed himself.

COVENT-GARDEN THEATRE.

14th *September* 1767.

FROM the Death of Mr. *Rich* in *December* 1762, to the above Period, this Theatre was under the Direction of Mr. *Beard*, his Son-in-law, by the Appointment of the Widow, and the reft of the Parties concerned—(Mr. *Rich* leaving (befides his Widow) four Daughters all then living and married, and an equal Dividend to be made amongft them) Mr. *Beard* being a Man of a refpectable Character, and bred to Mufic—he very naturally and judicioufly exerted his Powers to diftinguifh that Theatre by mufical Performances, as his Predeceffor had done

by

by Pantomime :—In short, as he had no eminent Actors, and Mr. *Garrick* in his Zenith at *Drury-Lane* Theatre, there was no other, or wiser Course to take, and therefore the best Singers and musical Performers were engaged :—Mr. *Rich* left them the *Coronation* to begin with, which brought several crouded Houses:—then appeared *Love in a Village*—*Artaxerxes*—the *Maid of the Mill*, &c. the great Success that attended all these musical Performances, sufficiently justified the Conduct of the Manager; and thus it continued for four very prosperous Years—I believe the fifth began to abate :—That Hint, and another (more sensibly felt) Mr. *Beard*'s *deafness*, with which he was then troubled to a mortifying Degree, for a musical Performer, brought the Sale of the Patent once more forward, which Purchase was completed,

and

and Sixty thousand Pounds paid down in *August* 1767—by four very enterprising young Men, especially as three of them were to be Gentlemen at large—and two unacquainted with the Business and Conduct of a Theatre.

Thus *general'd* was this Theatre opened on the above Day with the Comedy of the *Rehearsal*, under the Management of Mr. *Colman*, Mr. *Harris*, Mr. *Rutherford*, and Mr. *Powell*.—But the three last Gentlemen had the Prudence to assign over the Conduct of the Stage to Mr. *Colman*, who, as a Scholar, and a successful Dramatic Author, had the best Right to it.

The first new Performance exhibited this Season, was,

Nov.

LYCIDAS, an Elegy, set to Music by Mr. *Jackson* of *Exeter*—well executed,

executed, and well intended by him, as a Condolance on the much-lamented Death of the DUKE OF YORK—it was performed the Night after his Funeral—and that Night only.

This fine Poem was wrote by *Milton*, in his Bloom of Youth and Genius, occafioned by the Death of a Companion of great Worth and Merit, who was drowned in his Paffage to *Ireland*.

But any mournful Ditty muft be unfit for a Theatrical Entertainment to follow a Play; where no Subject but Mirth or Shew! and no Mufic but the Ballad or facetious Burletta, can ftand any Chance for Succefs.

THE IRISH FINE LADY, a Farce, by Mr. *Maclin*.

This fine Lady was so ill used by the Audience the first Night, that she never appeared afterwards.

THE OXONIAN IN TOWN, a Comedy of two Acts, by *George Colman*, Esq.

This little Comedy was violently opposed by a Party, at whom the Satire of this Piece was supposed to be levelled:— But as they were not well supported, and too well known, they failed in their Attempt; it was then perform'd several Nights with Success.

THE ROYAL MERCHANT, an Opera.

It

It was said in the Bills, and Title Page of the printed Copy, *founded on Beaumont and Fletcher.* It was founded indeed—as every Scene was taken (with some little Alteration) from their *Beggar's Bush*; and occasional Songs added where the Editor thought proper. As much Merit as can be claimed for some very pretty Sonnets is due to the Author of them.

25th *Jan.* 1768.

THE GOOD NATUR'D MAN, a Comedy, by *Doctor Goldsmith.*

The low Scenes in this Comedy, though naturally (perhaps too naturally) written, were dislik'd by the Audience the first Night, and after that omitted in the

the Performance; some of the Characters are well drawn, particularly that of *Croker* (an Original) and happily suited to the Powers of the Actor. Some of the Incidents are truly Comic, which secured deserved Success to this Comedy; with all its Errors it appeared to be written by a Man of Genius, not sufficiently practised in Dramatic Writing; the Public is therefore in great Expectation of having a complete Comedy from this Author.

KING LEAR, altered by *George Colman*, Esq.

The Intent of this Alteration was, to clear this celebrated Tragedy from the Love Scenes of *Edgar*

Edgar and *Cordelia*, which were introduced into this Play by the Poet Laureat Mr. *Tate*.—This Love Bufinefs has been ever ridiculed by the Connoiffeurs and Admirers of *Shakefpear*; and yet when the above Alteration was performed, the Play-going People, in general, feemed to lament the Lofs of thofe Lovers in the Reprefentation.

LIONEL AND CLARISSA, a Dramatic, Comic Opera, by Mr. *Bickerftaff*.

This Performance met with a favourable Reception from the Public, but in a much inferior Degree than the *Love in a Village*, or *Maid of the Mill*, of this Author.

On the 23d of *May* 1768, died Mr. PALMER, in the Fortieth Year of his Age.

Since the Days of the celebrated Mr. *Wilks*, moſt of our genteel Comedies have ſuffered by the Loſs of Actors, to ſupply the Characters of well-bred Gentlemen:— And as ſo few well-faſhion'd, accompliſh'd, young Men have offered themſelves to the Stage ſince that Period, the Loſs even of Mr. *Palmer* was not eaſily ſupplied.

The Mention of Mr. *Wilks* in the fine Gentlemen, reminds me of a Criticiſm I have lately heard, *viz.* A certain Minutiæ in his Action, that he was guilty of in moſt of his principal Characters—as his *Sir Charles Eaſy*, in the Scene where he is ſitting with his Wife, in a Converſation not very agreeable to him—and to ſhew his Negligence, he always in one particular Speech was altering the Role of his Stocking;— " The Man (ſays the Critic) who could
" act

"act so mechanically, must certainly want "Genius."

The Charge, I believe, is true—He did so—and it might be a Proof of his real Want of Genius—but he had an agreeable Form, and by Nature (improved by Art) the most easy, elegant, Deportment that ever Actor appeared with! He played several of the tender Parts of Tragedy with Success, though with great Singularity; but from his Energy, and exquisite Feelings, he never failed to make his Audience *feel him*, effectually.

I cannot help, in this Place, and on this Occasion, reflecting on the Loss the Stage had the Misfortune to sustain by the Absence of Mr. *O'Brien!* who was the nearest the Mark I have seen (or ever expect to see) in his easy, elegant Deportment in genteel Comedy.

In the Month of *August* following, the Stage suffered an almost irreparable Loss, by the Death of that excellent Actress, *Mrs.* PRITCHARD, at the Age of Fifty-seven.

She was engaged by the Managers of *Drury-Lane* Theatre in the Year 1732: but very soon after that Theatre (by Purchase) falling into other Hands, great Revolutions and Distress ensued, and remained so some Time :—When the Patent (by a second Purchase) came into the Hands of *Charles Fleetwood,* Esq.—something like Regularity and Decorum was restored to the Stage, and Performers of Merit began to come forward; in that List Mrs. *Pritchard* appeared in the Character of *Rosalind,* and gave universal Satisfaction to many delighted Audiences.—Soon after she revived and exhibited the Charms of the departed

departed *Oldfield*, in the *Maria*, in *Cibber*'s *Nonjuror*—Her excellent Performance of that Character gave her the full Poſſeſſion of all the capital Parts in our genteel Comedies.—And though ſhe was well received, and juſtly applauded in all, yet her chief Excellence certainly lay in the natural, ſprightly, and what are called the *higher Characters in Comedy*: They who have ſeen her in *Roſalind*, *Mrs. Sullen*, *Lady Brute*, *Eſtifania*, *Clarinda*, and *Beatrice*, &c. will bear Teſtimony to what I ſay: In the laſt Part particularly, and in *Clarinda*, I have ſeen her *Ranger* and *Benedict* hard put to it (and they were thought not to want Spirit) to return the Ball of Repartee to her.

It may perhaps be ſaid to the Praiſe of Mrs. *Pritchard*, that ſhe could not enter into the Characters of Affectation with the ſame Degree of Excellence, as ſhe did thoſe

those of genuine, sprightly, unaffected Nature.

Though she could do nothing ill, yet there always seemed a Restraint upon her Genius, when she appeared in such Parts as *Clarissa in the Confederacy*, and *Lady Dainty* in the *Double Gallant*. In them she only shewed her great Knowledge in her Business, but in the others I have mentioned, her Genius shone out in the greatest Splendor.

I am now to speak of Mrs. *Pritchard*'s Abilities in Tragedy; and as my Design through this whole Work, is to be impartial, I will not scruple to declare, that though she was always deservedly applauded in *Tragedy*, and has performed in all the principal Characters with great Reputation, yet her Merit there was only not equal to the Powers she exhibited in *Comedy*: In *this* she never had, in the other she might have, a *Superior*; and yet, in the last Character she play'd, *Lady Macbeth*, and many others, we may long wish before we shall see her outdone.

Mrs. *Pritchard* was Thirty-seven Years on the Stage; and though for the last Twenty, she has been in Figure more than what the *French* call *en bon point*, yet she never lost her Ease and Vivacity. When young, she was of a slim Make, and though not a Beauty, she had a most agreeable Face, with very expressive Eyes! and the most articulate harmonious Voice that ever Woman was blest with.—Her *Conduct* and Movement on the Stage was easy, and elegant! in private Life it was exemplary! and worthy Imitation! She came to the Stage a married Woman——young and handsome! and very soon had a large Family

mily of Children, whom she brought up with the utmost Care and Attention;—and to the great Honour of the Theatre, and the Profession of an Actress, she went to the Grave, with an irreproachable, unblemished Character.

I cannot quit this Subject without presenting my Reader, with the last Lines she spoke on the Stage on her Benefit Night; *Macbeth*, which Mr. *Garrick* performed out of Respect to her, and was crouded with the first People of Distinction, at advanced Prices——and call'd her farewel Epilogue.

" The Curtain dropt—my mimic Life is past——
" That Scene of † Sleep and Terror was my last.
" Could I in such a Scene my Exit make,
" When ev'ry *real* Feeling was awake?
" Which beating *here*, superior to all Art,
" Bursts in full Tides from a most grateful Heart.

---

† The last Scene of LADY MACBETH.

" I now

" I now appear myself—distress'd, dismay'd,.
" More than in all the Characters I've play'd;
" In acted Passion, Tears must *seem* to flow;
" *But I have that within that passeth Show.*
" Before I go, and this lov'd Spot forsake,
" What Gratitude can give, my *Wishes* take;
" Upon your Hearts may no Affliction prey,
" Which cannot by the Stage be chas'd away;
" And may the Stage to please each virtuous Mind,
" Grow ev'ry Day more moral, more refin'd:
" Refin'd from Grossness—not by *foreign* Skill;
" Weed out the Poison—but be ENGLISH still!
  " To all my Brethren whom I leave behind,
  " Still may your Bounty—as to me—be kind;
  " To me, for many Years your Favours flow'd;
  " Humbly receiv'd—on small Desert bestow'd;
  " For which I feel—what cannot be exprest——
  " *Words* are too *weak*,—my *Tears* must speak
    " the rest."

DRURY-LANE THEATRE.

3d *Oct.* 1768.

THE PADLOCK, a Dramatic Opera, of two Acts, by Mr. BICKERSTAFF.

This Author in his Advertisement printed before the Opera, tells the Reader, he took the Fable, with all the Characters, unaltered, from a *Spanish* Novel, wrote by the celebrated *Cervantes*, Author of *Don Quixote:* This little Opera was received with general Applause, and performed Fifty-three Nights to crouded

crouded Houses. It was well acted; and without the Aid of Music, would have been an agreeable petite Piece—but with the Music (which was happily adapted, and well executed) it proved the most pleasing Entertainment. Mrs. ARNE's Youth, and innocent Appearance, added to her powerful Voice, and engaging manner of Singing, gave universal Delight—and the Part of MUNGO by Mr. DIBDIN, is as complete a low Character as ever was exhibited. It would be doing Injustice to this Genius, not to observe, that he was also the Composer of the well-adapted Music, to this very successful Performance.

17th *November.*

THE HYPOCRITE, a Comedy, taken from *Moliere* and *Cibber*, by the fame Author.

Mr. *Cibber*, about the Year 1717, brought his Comedy of the NONJUROR on the Stage, taken from the TARTUFFE of *Moliere*—which the Editor fays in his Preface to the *Hypocrite*, " *Being written to expofe a Party,* " *it was no longer interefting, be-* " *caufe the Folly, and Roguery it* " *defigned to ridicule no longer* " *exifted.*"

The *Nonjuror* was an acknowledged Government Play, written to expofe that particular Set of Men, who called themfelves PROTESTANTS, and yet *refufed to take the Oaths of Allegiance to* GEORGE *the Firft!*

First! upon the Eftablifhment of the Hanover Family on the *Englifh Throne!* The formidable Rebellion in *Scotland*, in the firft Year of the Reign of that King, by the *Papifts, Jacobites, Nonjurors,* and *Tories* of thofe Days, gave a Fable to *Cibber*, and a future Fortune, by the Succefs of this Comedy; which was greatly fupported by the Whigs, the *firm Friends to the Proteftant Succeffion!*

That Author obferves, in his excellent Apology for his Life, printed in the Year 1740, " *That the Bread he then eat as Poet Laureat, was owing to his writing the Nonjuror!* But as thofe abfurd People are no more—and as the Defcendants of thofe *Tories*, who drew the Sword againft the firft King of this Family, are now become great Loyalists! I agree with my Friend Mr. Bickerstaff, that the evil

evil Deeds of thofe Days fhould be forgotten! and all Party-Plays (except in an Exigence like that) fhould be exploded, and for ever banifhed from the Stage.

Mr. *Bickerſtaff* has preferved the MARIA of *Cibber* (which is certainly one of the moſt agreeable Coquets that ever was drawn) and two or three other Characters entire: As for thofe he has added, as they are meant to expofe the prefent Race of Hypocrites, they deferved the Succefs they met with, as they were well acted, and well received by many Audiences this Seafon.

This Author has thought proper in his Preface, to pay a particular Compliment to Mrs. *Abington*, and Mr. *King*, for their excellent Performances.

I remember the original Mrs. OLDFIELD in the *Maria*, and twenty-four Years ago

the

the *Nonjuror* was revived at both Theatres at the same Time, for the late Mrs. *Pritchard*, and Mrs. *Woffington*—and the Critics were greatly divided in their Opinion of the *Maria!* They had both their different Degrees of Excellence. Mrs. *Abington* has proved herself in that difficult Stile of Acting a *Genius*. And, what is fortunate for her, she had no one to imitate—and has no Rival.

Decemb. 17th.

ZINGIS, a Tragedy, by *Alexander Dow*, Esq.

  This Author is a Soldier, as we are told by the following Couplet in the Prologue, written by his Friend Mr. *Home*.

" But though he liv'd amidst the Cannons Roar,
" Thunder, like yours, he never fac'd before!"

  From his Station as an Officer
           in

in the *East Indies*, he had an Opportunity to entertain the Public with the agreeable Accounts of that Part of the Globe, under the Title of the History of *Hindostan*; he also employed himself in collecting Materials there for this Tragedy of *Zingis*, which, he says, is taken from the *Tarich Moguliftan*, or History of the *Mogul Tartars*, written in the *Persian* Language.

Though in the Sentiment and Diction of this Tragedy, there are many Beauties, yet the Audience laboured under some Perplexities, from the many hard Names, and technical Terms of the Tribes, and the Manners of the People, and Scene of Action

were

were removed too far from us, to be much interested in their Disasters; yet under these Disadvantages, this Tragedy met with a favourable Reception, and was performed Twelve Nights.

20th *Jan.* 1769.
WIT's LAST STAKE, a Farce of two Acts, taken from the *French*, by Mr. *King*, Comedian, and performed several Nights with Success.

Many of the *French* Comedies (from one of which this Farce is taken) are founded on that melancholy Absurdity, of infirm, dying, old Men, designing to marry young Women of Fortune —but the Incidents in this Piece are

are truly farcical, and greatly heightened, by this Author's agreeable Performance in it.

Feb. 4th.

THE SCHOOL FOR RAKES, a Comedy, by Mrs. GRIFFITH.

My agreeable Friend has dedicated this Play to Mr. *Garrick*, from the beft of Motives, GRATITUDE, for the great Services he did her, in furmounting thofe Difficulties fhe met with in her Fable! The *French* Author, Monfieur *Beaumarchais*, in his Comedy of *Eugenie* was too national, and confufed in the Conduct of his Characters, to ftand the leaft Chance for Succefs on the *Englifh* Stage—and though there may yet remain too much for the

morofe

morose Critic to employ his severer Talents; yet the Story is interesting—the Dialogue easy—and the Sentiments elegant and natural. It was performed only thirteen Nights, on Account of the approaching Benefits, and every Audience expressed their Approbation——a sure Prognostic of its being (in the Stage Phrase) a Stock Play.

Feb. 23d.

THE FATAL DISCOVERY, a Tragedy, performed several Nights with Success—greatly owing to the Persons who acted in it, particularly Mr. and Mrs. *Barry*, late Mrs. *Dancer*. The Author of this Tragedy thought proper to con-

conceal himself; but those who are Admirers of DOUGLAS, may easily find similar Strokes of Nature break out in the Stile and Sentiment.

Mrs. CLIVE, long the Darling of the Public, gave Notice to the Managers of her Design of quitting the Stage, and taking her Leave of the Town on her approaching Benefit Night—which was the 24th of *April* 1769.—Mr. *Garrick*, on this Occasion, politely offered the Service of his performing that Night, to shew his Respect to so capital a Performer. The Play was the WONDER, and LETHE.—All the Pit was taken into the Boxes, and not half large enough to answer the Demand for Places—so numerous, and so brilliant, was the Audience on that singular Occasion.— After the Play was over, Mrs. *Clive* addressed

dressed the Audience with the following Epilogue, written by her honourable Friend and Neighbour—Mr. WALPOLE.

With Glory satiate, from the bustling Stage,
Still in his Prime—and much about my Age,
Imperial CHARLES (if ROBERTSON says true)
Retiring, bade the jarring World adieu!
Thus I, long honoured with your partial Praise,
(A Debt my swelling Heart with Tears repays!
—Scarce can I speak—forgive the grateful Pause)
Resign the noblest Triumph, your Applause.
Content with humble Means, yet proud to own,
I owe my Pittance to your Smiles alone;
To private Shades I bear the golden Prize,
The Meed of Favour in a Nation's Eyes;
A Nation brave, and sensible, and free——
Poor CHARLES! how little when compar'd to me!
His mad Ambition had disturb'd the Globe,
And sanguine which he quitted was the Robe.
Too blest, cou'd he have dar'd to tell Mankind,
 When Pow'r's full goblet he forbore to quaff,
That conscious of Benevolence of Mind,
 For thirty Years he had but made them laugh.

Ill was that Mind with sweet Retirement pleas'd,
The very Cloister that he sought he teaz'd;
And sick, at once, both of himself and Peace,
He died a Martyr to unwelcome Ease.
Here ends the Parallel——my generous Friends,
My Exit no such tragic Fate attends;
I will not die—let no vain Panic seize you——
If I repent—I'll come again and please you.

Though it was my Intention through this Work, to avoid attempting to draw the Characters of Theatrical Performers, 'till they were in their Graves—yet, as I am advancing so near the End of my own Life, and having no small Reason to fear my old *Theatrical Acquaintance* may outlive me—I am tempted to indulge myself in the following Sketch of Mrs. *Clive*'s Character, which I hope will not be unacceptable to my Readers, at least to those who had not the Delight of seeing her excellent Performances.——I cannot

better

better introduce this Lady, than by the following Lines from MILTON.

> " Hafte thee, Nymph, and bring with thee
> " Jeft, and youthful Jollity——
> " Quips, and Cranks, and wanton Wiles,
> " Nods, and Becks, and wreathed Smiles——
> " *Sports*, that wrinkled Care derides,
> " And *Laughter*, holding both his Sides."

If ever there were a true Comic Genius, Mrs. CLIVE was one! She, perhaps, never was equalled in her Walk (as the Stage Term is) we are convinced, never excelled! She was always inimitable whenever fhe appeared in ftrong mark'd Characters of *middle*, or *low* Life—her NELL in the *Devil to pay* was Nature itfelf!—And the Spirit, Roguery, and fpeaking Looks of her Chamber-maids, accompanied with the moft expreffive Voice that ever fatisfied the Ears of an Audience, has made her Lofs irreparable!

As strong Humour is the great characteristic Mark of an *English* Comedy, so was it of this Laughter-loving, Joy-exciting Actress!—To enumerate the different Parts in which she excelled, would be feebly describing, what the Audiences have felt so powerfully—her extraordinary Talents could even raise a Dramatic *Trifle*, provided there was Nature in it, to a Character of Importance—Witness the *fine Lady* in LETHE, and the yet smaller Part of *Lady Fuz*, in the *Peep behind the Curtain* —such Sketches in her Hands became high finished Pictures!——But—that I may not be thought too partial to this favourite Comedian, I will venture to assert, she could not reach the higher Characters in Comedy, though she was ever excellent in the Affectation of them: When the High-life polish of Elegance was to appear

in

in all the confcious Superiority of a *Lady Townly*, I cannot fay that Mrs. *Clive* would have done Juftice to herfelf, or the Character—but had the leaft affected Imitation of that Character appeared upon the Stage, her Merit would, in Proportion, have been equal to that of Mrs. *Oldfield*'s! To fhew the great Power of the Actrefs in queftion —I fhall give an Inftance of it, where fhe forced, the whole Town to follow, and applaud her in a Character, which fhe certainly did not perform as the Author intended it—but which could not be refifted, and gave high Entertainment to thofe Critics, who frankly acknowledged, they were mifled by the Talents of the Actrefs.—The Part I mean is PORTIA in the *Merchant of Venice*.—In the firft Place —*blank Verfe*—as it wants the Truth and Elegance of Nature, was not uttered by

Mrs.

Mrs. *Clive* with that delightful Spirit which she always gave to *Prose*; the *Lawyer*'s Scene of *Portia* (as it is called) in the fourth Act, was certainly meant by *Shakespear*, to be *solemn, pathetic,* and *affecting*—the Circumstances must make it so—and therefore the Comic Finishing which Mrs. *Clive* gave to the different Parts of the Pleadings (though greatly Comic) was not in Character.

If therefore this Theatrical Genius was able to entertain, contrary to the Intention of the Author—what must we say of her, or what Words can describe her Merits, when she appeared in the Fulness of her Powers, and was the very Person she represented?

THEATRE ROYAL

COVENT-GARDEN.

3d *Decemb.* 1768.

CYRUS, a Tragedy, by Mr. *Hoole*, taken from *Metaſtaſio*.

This Tragedy was performed ſeveral Nights with Applauſe; being greatly ſupported by the judicious and ſpirited Performances of Mrs. *Yates*, and Mr. *Powell*.

Jan. 14th 1769.

TOM JONES, a Dramatic Opera, by Mr. *Reed*, taken from the celebrated Novel of that Name, written by the late *Henry Fielding*,

ing, Efq.——This, Performance met with a favourable Reception.

February.

THE SISTER, a Comedy, by Mrs. *Lennox*. This Comedy was fo ill treated by the Audience the firſt Night, that the Authoreſs had Spirit enough to withdraw it from the Theatre.

This Lady has written ſeveral Pieces that have acknowledged Merit——and her own Novel called *Henrietta*, which was well received by the Public in that Form, was too cloſely copied in this Dramatic Performance.

I have known ſeveral of theſe Attempts, and moſt of them have failed of Succeſs:—And I will venture to ſay, the *Marianne* and *Paifan Parvenu* of *Marivaux*, though they are both filled with Characters, Situations, and Pleafantry in the Novels, yet thofe very Situations and Sentiments taken literally would appear too flat and infipid, when brought into Action on the Stage; fuch was the Fate of this Undertaking.—But I cannot quit this Subject without hoping that this Lady, who is univerfally allow'd to be one of our firft female Geniufes, will exert her Spirit and Talents, which cannot fail (notwithftanding the above Accident) to produce a fuccefsful Dramatic Performance:——For what may we not expect from the Pen which has given fuch

true

true Entertainment to the Public, in her Tranflations and Novels—particularly the *Female Quixote.*

In the Month of *July* 1769, Mr. WILLIAM POWELL died at *Briftol*; to which Place he was retired to perform with his Summer Company, at the new Theatre there, of which he was one of the Managers.

This extraordinary young Actor appeared at *Drury-Lane* Theatre, in *October* 1763, in the Character of *Philafter*, in a Tragedy of that Name, written by *Beaumont* and *Fletcher*—and altered by *George Colman*, Efq. This young Man was introduced by his Friend Mr. *Holland* to Mr. *Garrick*, and by him approved, and well inftructed in the Part of *Philafter*, two or three Months before that Gentleman fet out for *Italy*; and since the first Appearance of that great Actor in *Richard*, no Onset was ever so promising—and no Stage Adventurer ever gave more universal Satisfaction to the Audience than Mr. *Powell*.

Philaster brought many crouded Houses that Season, entirely owing to this young Actor's uncommon Success! He performed (too soon after) several of the most capital Characters, before he had Time to consider and study them properly!——— As it is the Duty of the Historian to give just Resemblances of deceased Performers, to the best of his Abilities—— this Portrait cannot be finished without Light and Shade!

Mr. *Powell* had great Feelings—and his Spirits (the common and most excusable indiscretion of Youth) like the hot, fiery Steed, would too often run him out of the

the Courfe! He would then (as *Shakefpear* fays) a little *o'erftep the Modefty of Nature*. But (had not the Stage fuffer'd fo great a Lofs) *Time* and *Attention* to his Bufinefs would have corrected his youthful Errors: —He would then have been as judicious in his Execution, as he was exquifite in his Feelings!

In *September* 1767, he appeared at *Covent-Garden* Theatre, and opened that Seafon with a Prologue, wherein he declared himfelf an *Adventurous Manager!* Having paid down (by the Help of powerful Friends) fifteen thoufand Pounds for a fourth Part of that Patent! The Particulars of that Affair, the Public have been *more than fufficiently* informed of! Mr. *Powell* was, at that Time, bound in an Article to the Managers of *Drury-Lane* Theatre for three Years, in a Penalty of one thousand Pounds; which the Law would unquestionably have compelled him to pay, as the Damages sustained by his Defection were apparent.

He was attacked with a violent Fever at the Entrance of the Month of *June*, and died (after severe Sufferings) on the third of *July*, at the Age of Thirty-four. —He was buried in the College Church at *Bristol*, with great Funeral Honours, attended by the Dean and whole Choir, who sung an Anthem on that mournful Occasion. His Merits as an Actor, and an agreeable good natured Man, deserve the highest Commendations.

> N. B. The Author of a *Theatrical Register*, cannot possibly omit recording the most remarkable Occurrence that ever was known in this or any kingdom—I mean the JUBILEE at *Stratford*

Stratford upon Avon, in Honour of SHAKESPEAR! which lasted three Days, and began on the 7th of *September* 1769.——But as a regular Description of that very singular, superb Undertaking, must be of some Length—I shall refer the Reader, who has any Curiosity to satisfy, to the APPENDIX to this WORK.

THEATRE ROYAL

DRURY-LANE.

30th *September* 1769.

A N ODE on SHAKESPEAR, written and spoken by *David Garrick*, Efq. at the Jubilee at *Stratford upon Avon*—and was exhibited in the fame manner in *Drury-Lane* Theatre this Night, after the Comedy of the *Country Girl*. When the Curtain drew up, the Stage was difcovered, in the fame Form and Manner as at an Oratorio; in the Middle of the Front-line of Singers fat Mr. *Garrick*, who rofe to fpeak thofe Parts which in all mufical Performances are

the

the Recitative.—This agreeable Novelty had the defired Effect, and was received with conftant Plaudits from the Audience.— This Ode was performed feven Nights to crouded Houfes.——
The Mufic was compofed by Doctor *Arne*, and much admired.

14th *October*.

THE JUBILEE, a Dramatic, mufical Entertainment.

The Principal Characters in all *Shakefpear*'s Tragedies, and Comedies, with all their emblematic Trophies, were intended for a grand Pageant through the great Streets of *Stratford*, to the Amphitheatre on the fecond Day of the Jubilee, where the Ode

Ode was performed, and to be surrounded with all the Variety of *Shakespear*'s Characters—but the Weather proving remarkably rainy, this very pompous Spectacle was obstructed: Mr. *Garrick* (who had been at very great Expence and Trouble, in designing, and attempting to execute this superb Entertainment) when he had determined to introduce it on the Stage, soon found it necessary to form a Plan, and invent low Characters of Humour, to lengthen and explain some particular Parts of the Representation, which, with the Songs properly intermixed, gave Life and Spirit to the most magnificent Spectacle that ever

was

was exhibited on any Theatre !! And as a Proof of its Succefs with the Public, it was performed ninety-two Nights that Seafon, to crouded Houfes.

On the feventh Day of *December* 1769, Mr. CHARLES HOLLAND died of the fmall Pox, at the Age of Thirty-fix.

The Death of this very ufeful Actor, following fo clofe upon the Lofs of Mr. *Powell*, feemed, for a Time, to deftroy the Hopes of the rifing Generation, who have a natural Right to expect Entertainment from the Theatre.

Mr. *Holland* had great Requifites for a capital Actor; he had an agreeable, manly Appearance—with a ftrong, clear, well-ton'd, articulate Voice—and, by the Help of a good Underftanding, and great Attention to his Bufinefs, he made

made no small Amends for the want of Genius, if the Critics were right in their Observation; thus by Industry and Application, he became the best Copyer of Excellence that we shall see on the Stage for some Time.

I remember a parallel Case to this, many Years ago, among the portrait Painters.

Mr. *Dahl* held some Degree of Reputation, as a Portrait Painter, in Sir *Godfrey Kneller*'s Time; and though there was no Degree of Comparison to be made between their Merit—yet when Mr. *Dahl* was employed (as he often was) to copy a Portrait of Sir *Godfrey*'s, it required great Discernment to know the Difference between the Copy and the Original.

I wish I could say as much for Mr. *Holland*, when he appeared in *Hamlet* :— but, with all his Defects—he was a very useful

useful Actor—a very creditable Member of the Society, and his Death a great Loss to the Theatre, and to the Managers, to whom he was firmly attached from his first Establishment as an Actor, without the least Desire of changing his Situation.

It is said Mr. *Holland*'s Relations have obtained Leave from his Grace the Duke of *Devonshire*, at the Request of Mr. *Garrick*, to place a monumental *Inscription* in the Chancel of *Chiswick* Church, to the Memory of this Actor; and that it is to be written by the *Manager*, who best knew his Worth and Abilities.

Jan. 6th 1770.

A TRIP TO SCOTLAND, a Farce of two Acts, by *William Whitehead*, Esq.

This little Piece was well received; the Mischief it attacks is is pleasantly ridiculed—the Satire is just, and the Design well executed, and original.

8th *February*:

LIONEL AND CLARISSA, OR THE SCHOOL FOR FATHERS; a Comic Opera.

Mr. *Bickerstaff*, the Author of *Lionel* and *Clarissa*, as first performed at *Covent Garden* Theatre, has improved it by Alterations, Additions, and given it a compound Title. The Fable as it now stands is very interesting, and the whole Opera an agreeable Entertainment, and meets with general Approbation.

March 3d.

A WORD TO THE WISE, a Comedy, by Mr. *Hugh Kelly*.

The

The firſt Night's Audience to this Play were too conceited, and too wiſe, to hear one Word of additional Wiſdom from this Performance; and therefore the Merits of the Play were not attended to; nor any Thing taken into Conſideration, but the private Conduct of the Author, who was charged by his Opponents, with being a *miniſterial* PARTY WRITER!

The *Stage* has been often called the *Poetical Pillory!* And many a poor Author has been ſeverely pelted there. The Reader will eaſily ſee the unavoidable danger a *Dramatic* Author muſt run, who, in the midſt of Faction,

tion, is suppofed to be a *Party Writer!*

I am a Stranger to the Truth of this Charge againſt Mr. *Kelly*—he has endeavoured to exculpate himſelf from it, in a full and clear Preface to the Public, printed before his Comedy, which, though it never had a fair Hearing on the Stage, he was encouraged to publiſh by a very large Subſcription.

COVENT-GARDEN THEATRE.

7th *Oct.* 1769.

MAN AND WIFE; or the *Shakespear's Jubilee*, a Comedy of two Acts, by *George Colman*, Esq.

The Jubilee at *Stratford upon Avon*, in Honour of *Shakespear*, which was celebrated there at the Entrance of the preceding Month, and was invented and conducted by Mr. *Garrick*, at great Expence and Trouble, furnished the Hint for this Piece, which Mr. *Colman* availed himself of, by bringing it on

Covent-

Covent-Garden Theatre, before that Exhibition at *Drury-Lane* could be got ready.

Though this Transaction has been differently spoken of, yet, it must be confessed to have been the practice Time immemorial, of the Managers of contending Theatres; this Entertainment was performed several Nights, and well received by the Public.

4th *November* 1769.

THE RAPE of PROSERPINE, with *the Birth and Adventures of Harlequin*, was revived at this Time, with the addition of two new Scenes—*viz.* a View of the Eruptions of *Mount Ætna*, and the other the *Palace of Pluto*.—

This

This laft famous Scene was defigned and executed by *Servandoni*, when he was in *London*, about thirty Years ago:—The late Mr. *Rich* (having eftablifhed his *Fame* and *Fortune* by *Pantomime*) was at all Times ready to embrace every Opportunity (at any Expence) that offered to the Ornament and Advantage of the *Harlequinade!* He therefore employed this celebrated *Italian* to paint this expenfive Set of Scenes—but having at that Time no Plan to exhibit them—he laid them by, like a wife General, as a Corps de referve.

The new Manager thought this a proper Time to introduce them, to oppofe the ftrong Current

rent of the Jubilee at the other House.—The judicious Public gave them due Praise: The Design was indeed a noble one—but surely the brilliancy of the Colours must have suffered by the Length of Time.

2d *December*.

THE BROTHERS, a Comedy.

It must be confessed the Author of this Comedy, who also wrote the Prologue, set out rather injudiciously, by a general Attack on all his Brethren of the Sock, as Pirates on the old *English* Authors, or Dependants on the *French* Comedies; and, at the same Time, promised a little too much for himself: This, of course, brought on the heaviest

heaviest Censures from his incensed Brethren, who were sure to give him no Quarter.

As to the Merits of the Comedy, I shall only observe it was performed several Nights, and met with a very favourable Reception from the Public.—As it is printed, every Reader has a Right to judge for himself; tho' there were many Criticisms upon this Comedy, yet the impartial Public had great Hopes of the Author, from the Variety of Characters in this Play.

15th.

AMYNTAS, an *English* Opera, collected and compiled from the *Italian* of *Metastasio*, and the *English* Translation called the *Royal Shep-*

Shepherd—the Mufic compofed by Mr. *Rufh*, from whom feveral Airs are taken; and the reft from the Works of different Mafters:——This occafional Medley was ferved up by Signior *Tenducci*, for his own Benefit Night.

5th *Jan.* 1770.

THE COURT of ALEXANDER, a Burlefque Opera, of two Acts, by *George Alexander Stevens*, the ingenious Author of the celebrated Lecture upon Heads.

The Humour of this Burlefque was, in general, thought too vulgar and low to be exhibited at a Theatre-Royal in *London.*

27th.

HARLEQUIN's JUBILEE, a Pantomime, by Mr. *Woodward.*

This Entertainment ſtood very little Chance for Succeſs, coming juſt after two Exhibitions on the Subject of the *Jubilee*, at each Theatre, both of which depended rather too much on *Pantomime.*

DRURY-LANE THEATRE.

IT's WELL IT's NO WORSE, a Comedy, by Mr. *Bickerstaff.*

The Author of this Comedy informs us in his Preface, that it was written by DON PEDRO CALDERON DE LA BARCA—— and that this very venerable Dramatic Writer was the Grandfather of moſt of our *Engliſh* Comedies—as the beſt *French* Authors tranſlated and pirated from him, and our *Engliſh* Dramatic Writers from the *French!*

As to the Comedy before us, it is (I preſume) as well tranſlated,

lated, improved, and adapted to the Manners of our Stage, as any of thofe Productions—it was alfo well acted in all its Parts— the Scenes and Decorations complete.—And, from the Spirit of the Intrigue, and Variety of Comic Incidents, the Attention of the Audience was well kept up to the End;—and tho' this Comedy was not as well approved, and fupported, as many Pieces have been from this Author, it was performed Eleven Nights.

To account for the Coldnefs of the Reception it met with from the Public—I fhould fay it was occafioned by the Want of due Diftinction in the Characters—becaufe as it now ftands, though there is Intrigue in its full Extent, and Variety of Comic Incidents, yet the Spectators were not fufficiently *interefted* in the Confequences that attend any of the Characters! And a capital, ftriking Scene or two (as in the *Wonder*, which is alfo taken from a *Spanifh* Novel) is wanting in this Comedy.

13th *December*.

KING ARTHUR, a Dramatic Opera.

This celebrated Performance was written by DRYDEN, and the Mufic compofed by PURCELL—two eminent Geniufes!

And yet, in this improved, enlightened Age, we are apt to laugh at feveral bombaftical Strokes,

Strokes, which I prefume were received with great Gravity by the firſt Audience to *King Arthur.* The following Couplet is one Inſtance.

Ofwald. (p. 21.) Act II.
" Or if I fall, make room, ye Bleſt above!
" For one who was undone and died for Love.

Purcell's Muſic retains its due Force and Merit, becauſe founded on Nature.—However the Revival of this Dramatic Opera has always anſwered the Expectations of every Adventurer—and the Managers who have Singers, are always right to have *King* ARTHUR in their Stock.— This Revival at *Drury-Lane* Theatre was ſure to anſwer the warmeſt Expectations, as the Managers were determined to ſpare

spare no Expence in the Scenery, and Decorations, to make it a superb Entertainment.

12th *Jan.* 1771.

ALMIDA, a Tragedy, written by a *Lady.*

This Tragedy has great Dramatic Requisites—and was received by the Audience with universal Applause, and has escaped the Censure of the Critic, perhaps, as the Performance of a Lady.—It was well acted in all its Parts—but, particularly, by Mrs. *Barry* in *Almida,* who (it was generally thought) excelled every Female that has appeared in that Theatre for many Years.

19th *January.*

THE WEST INDIAN, a Comedy, by *Richard Cumberland,* Esq. Author of of the *Summer's Tale*, and the *Brothers*.

This Comedy has fully anſwered the Expectations of the Public, from this improving, Dramatic Author. It has unqueſtioned Merit :—and though when critically compared, not quite equal to ſome few of our beſt Comedies, yet the Succeſs that has attended the Performance of the *Weſt-Indian*, has exceeded that of any Comedy within the Memory of the oldeſt Man living! There was the ſame Demand for Places in the Boxes, and the ſame crouding to get into the Pit and Galleries at the *twenty-ſixth* Repreſentation, as on the firſt Night!

THE RECRUITING SERJEANT, a musical Interlude.

This Piece was written by Mr. *Bickerstaff*, and set to Music by Mr. *Dibden*, for an Entertainment at *Ranelagh*, and was performed there:—and some necessary addition formed it into an agreeable Interlude to be introduced between the Play and Farce at the Theatre.

COVENT-GARDEN THEATRE.

26th *Decemb.* 1770.

MOTHER SHIPTON, a Pantomime.

This Performance was made remarkable by the Machenift.— Two or three Scenes are well invented, and well executed, which is fufficient to fecure Succefs.

In moft of the late Pantomimes, the *Harlequin*, who is the Hero— and always the fortunate Lover, does nothing but run away with his Miftrefs, and give Signals with his magical wooden Sword, to direct the Men to shift the Scenes, from one Form and Situation to another: In former Times *Harlequin* shewed his Agility, and made several difficult Escapes, that appeared to carry danger, and thereby alarm and surprize the Audience! But our modern *Harlequins* are determined to sleep in a whole Skin, and never venture a Leg but into the Lap of *Columbine*.

Upon Enquiry, I find that *Italy* claims the Honour of giving Birth to this motley *Being*, and his Brother *Scaramouch*—this last was always the Servant to the old *Father*, and the other to the *Son*, in most of their Dramatic

Dramatic Pieces—but he was a speaking Varlet; and always introduced as a blundering Servant, doing all the Mischief to his Master.—The *French* soon adopted him—and made him a Pimp of consequence.——The late Manager Mr. RICH, when young, went into that Character, under the feigned Name of *Lun*; he had the Ingenuity to strike out an *Harlequin* entirely his own:—His Genius was confined to Pantomime! and being a complete *Mimer*, he carried that Art to such Perfection, as to render Words needless to describe his Business, or his Meaning! That was *pantomiming* indeed! It was his amazing Powers that brought thofe Entertainments into Fafhion—which are now funk into nothing but nonfenfe and Exhibitions of fine Scenery—and (what has been long wifhed by all true Lovers of the Drama) will foon be treated with Contempt.

N. B. It may not be improper in this Place to obferve, that the Leaders of the laft Riot at both the Theatres, who called themfelves the Town, and did fo much Mifchief (with Impunity) to both Houfes, to compel the Managers to admit them after the third Act at Half-price, to every *New* as well as old Performance, *except the firft Seafon of a new Pantomime!* By that very wife Stipulation, they took the only method in

their

their Power to promote and eſtabliſh that ſhameful Exhibition long complained of, whilſt the Authors of four ingenious Dramatic Petite Pieces, *the Deuce is in him*, the *Peep behind the Curtain*, the *Padlock*, and *Trip to Scotland* (which have more Merit than ever was crammed into all the *Pantomimes* from their Creation) were ſeen the firſt Night, with two Acts of the Play, at *Half-price*, and *conſequently*, the Profits at the Authors Benefits, rendered trifling and precarious.

23d *Feb.* 1771.

CLEMENTINA, a Tragedy. Author unknown.

 This Tragedy met with a favourable Reception, and was performed Nine Nights.

27th *April*.

THE MODERN WIFE, a Comedy.

This is a Comedy of the late Mr. *Gay*'s, revived with some few Alterations, for the Benefit of Mrs. *Leſſingham*.

THE APPENDIX.

IN the Month of *July* 1766, a Royal PATENT was granted to SAMUEL FOOTE, Esq. to build a *Theatre* in the City and Liberties of *Westminster*, and to exhibit Dramatic Performances, &c. &c. therein, from the 14th Day of *May* to the 14th Day of *September*, during his natural Life.

This *Patentee* was born a Gentleman; and (what was more fortunate for him in his present Situation) with a Comic Genius of the first Class! which having been improved by a liberal Education, has enabled

enabled him to acquire a large, annual Income, by his own perfonal Merit:—and as he has Tafte and Spirit to enjoy it, no one becomes it with a better Grace.

Mr. *Foote* having purchafed the old Playhoufe in the *Hay-Market* (from the Executors of Mr. *Potter*, the Carpenter who built it in the Year 1720) he erected an entire new *Theatre* on that Ground, greatly enlarged, and opened it the *May* following.

2d *July* 1767.

The firft new Performance was
THE TAYLORS, a mock heroic Tragedy.

This Piece is founded upon a fimilar Plan to Sir *Samuel Garth*'s celebrated *Difpenfary*, and has very fingular Merit:— the great Commotions in *London*,

don, some time before, between the Master Taylors, and their Journeymen, gave a Subject to this facetious Author.——This Tragedy was sent to the Manager from Mr. *Dodsley*'s Shop, to try his Taste, and if not approved to return it there in the same concealed manner it came to him—But he knew its Worth too well, not to thank the Author for the Present. Mr. *Foote* soon ordered it into Rehearsal, and took the principal Part himself, which, from his Comic Powers, he was sure to make entertaining—and, indeed, several other Characters were well performed; for every strolling Tragedian cannot fail to make a pleaa pleasant Figure, and excel in mock Heroics: Thus this Tragedy gave Delight to several Audiences, and the expected Profit to the Manager.

Mr. *Garrick*, to shew his Friendship to Mr. *Foote*, and his Approbation of this excellent Piece of Humour, wrote a facetious Prologue to this mock heroic Piece.

THE COUNTESS OF SALISBURY, a Tragedy, by HALL HARTSTONE, Esq. at that Time a Student of Trinity College *Dublin*.

This Tragedy was performed at the Theatre-Royal in *Dublin* the preceding Winter—and Mr. *Barry*, and Mrs. *Dancer* being engaged

engaged with Mr. *Foote*, to act an agreed Set of Plays on Shares, during the Summer Seaſon,— they performed this Tragedy there ſeveral Nights with great Succeſs.

THEATRE-ROYAL

IN THE

HAY-MARKET.

30th *May* 1768.

THE DEVIL UPON TWO STICKS, a Dramatic Satire, by Mr. *Foote*. It has been thought by many, that this Performance having a Name in common with one written by the celebrated *Le Sage*, Author of *Gil Blas*, that it is an Imitation of the *Diable Boiteux*: this is a great Miftake, as there is not the leaft Similitude in the Plan, Characters, or Conduct of thofe two Pieces. Leaving the

French

French Novel, which has great Merit (though inferior to *Gil Blas*) I shall confine myself wholly to our *English* Original—an Original indeed! and which justly demands a much abler Pen than mine, to give an adequate Idea of its peculiar Excellence.

Though the Author has judiciously calculated the principal Part (*viz.* the *Devil*) to his own Circumstances, and manner of playing, yet, separated from that, and the Delusion of Representation, it has great Variety of Merit, and would afford to the Reader, were it printed, uncommon Entertainment.

To speak first of the Characters—his own—including the *political Doctor*, the *President of the College*, are never seen without the greatest Marks of Applause; and as they are supported by strong, Characteristic Wit and Humour, will be equally supported in the Closet.

Mr. FOOTE has produced some Characters, which, perhaps, would fail of the Effect from any Performer but himself—such as those which so much entertained the Town in his *Tea Exhibitions*, &c.—but the Dramatic Strength of Character in his *Devil upon two Sticks*, will be applauded, when the comic Powers of the Actor are no more.

We

We cannot omit in this Place, to give our small tribute of Praise to Mr. *Weston*, who performed the excellent Character of *Doctor Last*, in all the true Dramatic Simplicity with which it is written: It is not among the smallest of Mr. *Foote*'s Merits, that he has produced this Actor to the Public, and adapted Characters to his peculiar Talents; which has given him a Station among principal, low Comedians.

Dramatic Satires, in general, are only Beings of a certain Time, and live as long as the Objects of the temporary Satire exists—but when the Characters turn upon general Ridicule, and a *President* of a College, or *political Doctor*,

Doctor, will afford Laughter as well in the next Century as this, then the Performance becomes truly Dramatic, and will continue as long as we have the name of Humour amongſt us.— Add to all this, that the *Devil upon two Sticks*, unlike the general run of Dramatic Satires, has an intereſting Fable interwoven with it, and does not depend on ſingle detached Scenes.

Mr. *Foote*, at the End of this Piece, always gave ſome humorous Stroke of Satire, upon the Pleaſures, or Circumſtances of the Day—the *Bal paree* at *Ranelagh*—the *Ridotto al Freſco*, at *Vauxhall*—the *Diſputes of the Covent-Garden Managers*—and, above

above all, the *Stratford Jubilee*, and its *Author*—have, in their turns, been laughed at by this great Master of Ridicule! This generally finishes the Piece with universal Applause—and is so dexterously managed, that the Persons themselves who are the Objects of his Pleasantry, cannot help joining in the full Chorus of Laughter.

N. B. Lest the Critics should object to my having said, that there is no Similitude between the *Devil upon two Sticks*, and *le Diable Boiteux*, I must take notice of one trifling Circumstance that is common to both—the *Devil* in *le Sage* rises out of a Vial—but the *English Devil*, though equally

equally fpiritual, yet being fomewhat more corporeal, is obliged to make his Appearance out of a ten Gallon wicker Bottle.

THEATRE-ROYAL

IN THE

HAY-MARKET.

1769.

DOCTOR LAST IN HIS CHA-RIOT, a Comedy of three Acts, taken from *La Maladie imaginaire* of *Moliere*, and intended as a Sequel to the *Devil upon two Sticks*.——The first Night's Audience seemed greatly inclined to overturn *Doctor Last* in his Chariot; and behaved so refractory, as to oblige Mr. *Foote* to address them in the following manner.

" That

"That the Comedy which they were pleased to treat so severely, was written by a Gentleman who had enjoyed the frequent Pleasure of entertaining the Public with some of their favourite Pieces, and therefore he thought he had a Right to a fair Trial in his Theatre—which if they would please to permit, the Exceptions they should make, should be struck out, or altered against the next Performance."

This Request appeared so reasonable, that the rational Part of the Audience readily complied with it, and the Actors went through the Comedy, with some little Obstructions—but the general

neral Opinion was, *that it would be short liv'd.*

I remember going into the House at the second Performance, about the middle of the Play, and found the House not only well filled, but the whole Audience in good Humour, and laughing through every Scene of the Comedy—which was continued to ten or twelve Nights.

THE CAPTIVE, a Comic Opera.

This little Piece is taken from a Comic Episode in *Don Sebastian*, written by *Dryden*, and met with no great Success.

THEATRE-ROYAL
IN THE
HAY-MARKET.

1770.

THE LAME LOVER, a Comedy of three Acts, by Mr. *Foote*.

This must also be called a *Dramatic Satire*; but the Question now is, whether it turns upon *general* Ridicule? Because it was said to be drawn for a particular Person—and that a *Misfortune* was not a proper Subject for Ridicule.——Every Man under a real Misfortune has an undoubted Claim to our Com-

Compaſſion:—but if that Man will ſo far forget it, as vainly to endeavour to conceal, and ornament that Blemiſh, and give himſelf ſuch Airs as would have diſgraced him, when his Perſon was perfect—ſurely he becomes then a proper Object for the Satiriſt? The Public, when the Party is of conſequence enough to be generally known, are the proper Judges in this Caſe.

I ſhall therefore only obſerve, that the *Lame Lover* was well adapted to the Comic Powers of Mr. *Foote*—and the Performance met with general Applauſe from many crouded Audiences.

AS a Theatrical Hiftorian, I cannot omit recording the moft remarkable Event that ever happened in the Annals of *Theatres*, fince the firft Eftablifhment of Dramatic Poetry in *Europe*, or, perhaps, in the known World; I mean the JUBILEE AT STRATFORD UPON AVON, which was exhibited three Days fucceffively, on the fixth, feventh, and eighth of *September* 1769—in Honour of the immortal SHAKESPEARE! that being the Town where he was born and educated.

The common Obfervation, that great Events have arifen from fmall Beginnings, was never more verified than in the Progrefs of SHAKESPEARE's JUBILEE! It will, perhaps, not be difagreeable to the Reader, that I take this Matter a little earlier,

and

and mention an Accident which happened fome few Years before in this Town of *Stratford*.——A certain Clergyman had purchafed fome Property in and about this Town, and with it the Houfe which was *Shakefpeare*'s—in the Garden of this Houfe there was a remarkable MULBERRY TREE, which the Inhabitants looked upon with Veneration, as it was planted by *Shakefpeare*'s own Hand.—The Gentleman to whom the Houfe and Garden belonged, finding that the Tree overfhadowed too much of the Houfe, and made it damp, not having the Fear of his Neighbours before his Eyes, or the Love of *Shakefpeare* in his Heart! one unlucky Night moft facrilegioufly cut it down! The Alarm of this horrid Deed foon fpread through the Town!—Not the going out of the *Veftal Fire* at old *Rome*, or the ftealing away the

K 5 *Palladium*

Palladium from old *Troy*, could more have aſtoniſhed *Romans* and *Trojans*, than this horrid Deed did the Men, Women, and Children of old *Stratford!* After the firſt moments of Aſtoniſhment were over, a general Fury ſeized them all, and Vengeance was the Word!—They gathered together, ſurrounded the Houſe—reviewed with Tears the fallen Tree, and vowed to ſacrifice the Offender, to the immortal Memory of the Planter! In ſhort, ſuch a Spirit was on Foot, that the Clergyman, after conſulting with his Friends, and ſkulking from Place to Place, was perſuaded to quit the Town, where he never would have been permitted to abide in Peace—and where all the Inhabitants have moſt religiouſly reſolved never to ſuffer any one of the ſame Name to dwell amongſt them.

The

The *Mulberry Tree* was inftantly bought up, and the Purchafer, who was a Carpenter, retail'd and cut out the Branches of it into various Relicks, of Stand-difhes, Tea-chefts, Inkhorns, Tobacco Stoppers, &c. &c. &c.—The *Corporation of Stratford* fecured fome of the beft Part of it:—and among other Fancies which this facred Tree gave rife to, the moft remarkable was the following Letter, written by their Steward to Mr. *Garrick*, that began to lay the Foundation of the celebrated *Shakefpeare Jubilee*, which is the Subject of the following Pages.

An Extract of the Steward's Letter to Mr. Garrick.

"The *Corporation of Stratford*, ever
"desirous of expressing their Gratitude
"to all who do Honour and Justice to
"the Memory of *Shakespeare*, and highly
"sensible that no Person, in any Age,
"hath excelled You therein, would think
"themselves much honoured if you would
"become one of their Body: though this
"Borough doth not now send Members
"to Parliament, perhaps the Inhabitants
"may not be less virtuous; and to render
"the *Freedom* of this Place the more ac-
"ceptable to *you*, the *Corporation* propose
"to send it in a Box made of that very
"*Mulberry Tree*, planted by *Shakespeare*'s
"own Hand—The Story of that valuable
"Relick is too long to be here inserted—
"but

" but the Gentleman who is so obliging as
" to convey this to you, will acquaint you
" therewith.—As also that the Corporation
" would be happy in receiving from your
" Hands, some Statue, Bust, or Picture
" of *Shakespeare*, to be placed within their
" new Town-hall.—They would be equal-
" ly pleased to have some Picture of your-
" self, that the Memory of both may be
" perpetuated together in that Place which
" gave him Birth, and where he still lives
" in the Mind of every Inhabitant.

" I am, Sir, &c."

This pleasing Honour, so judiciously conferred, wrought so powerfully on the Mind of this inspired Actor, that he soon formed a Scheme for a JUBILEE at STRATFORD! which (when known) engaged the Attention of all that Part of the Kingdom, that lay within one hundred Miles of the Place

Place of Action—and, at the laſt Play performed at the Theatre Royal that Seaſon for the Benefit of *the Fund for decayed Actors*, Mr. *Garrick* cloſed it with the following Addreſs to the Audience, by way of Invitation to the *Jubilee*.

After taking Leave of the Audience, and ſaying at the End of the Epilogue—
" next Year we come again;

[*bowing to the Audience.*
" My Eyes, 'till then, no Sights like this will ſee,
" Unleſs we meet at *Shakeſpeare's Jubilee!*
" On Avon's *Banks where Flowers eternal blow!*
" Like its full Stream our Gratitude ſhall flow!
" There let us revel, ſhew our fond Regard,
" On that lov'd Spot, firſt breath'd our *matchleſs* Bard;
" To Him all Honour, Gratitude is due,
" To Him we owe our All—to *Him*, and *You*."

When the Plan was formed, and agreed upon, amongſt other expenſive Orders, the moſt conſiderable was the Amphitheatre to be erected, on the Model of that in *Ranelagh Gardens*, for the Public Performances and Balls, in the Mornings

and

and Evenings—and in the middle of the Day to entertain the whole Body of Nobility and Gentry assembled on that Occasion, at a public Ordinary.

The Painters not only decorated the AMPHITHEATRE with various Devices, but they also prepared several excellent Transparences for the *Town-hall* Windows, in which the most striking Tragic and Comic Characters in *Shakespeare's* Plays were exhibited;—this had a most agreeable Effect at Night, when the whole *Town* was illuminated.——A very small old House in which this great Poet was born, was covered with a curious Transparency—the Subject was the SUN struggling through Clouds to enlighten the World, in which was figuratively delineated the low Circumstances of *Shakespeare*, from which his Strength of Genius rais'd him, to become the *Glory of his Country!*

In

In the Procession it was intended that they should stop at that hallowed Spot, and sing an Air, which began with these Lines,

> " From Clouds he broke forth,
> " To enlighten the Earth!
> " And spread all his Glory around"——

This public Building, with other various necessary Preparations to execute this great Plan, unavoidably drove the Day of Action to the sixth Day of *September*, which was one Month too late.

When the Morning's dawn broke forth, the whole Town was alarmed with the discharge of several Pieces of Cannon—soon after a Troop of Singers appeared in the Streets, in masquerade Habits, with Gittars, and other Instruments, to serenade the most remarkable Personages that were come to honour the Jubilee! Before each
House

House they sung the following Song in full Chorus:

(I.)

Let Beauty with the Sun arise!
To *Shakespeare* Tribute pay!
With heav'nly Smile, and speaking Eyes,
Give Lustre to the Day!

(II.)

Each Smile she gives protects his Name,
What Face shall dare to frown?
Not Envy's self can blast the Fame,
Which Beauty deigns to crown.

When that was over, printed Handbills were left at every House, to inform the Company of the various Entertainments, for the different Parts of the Day and Night.

FIRST DAY,

Wednesday the 6th of *September*.

SHAKESPEARE's JUBILEE.

The Steward of the Jubilee begs Leave to inform the COMPANY,

that, at Nine o'Clock will be a
PUBLIC BREAKFAST
at the Town Hall:
Hence to proceed to the Church to hear
The ORATORIO of JUDITH,
which will begin exactly at Eleven.
From Church will be a full *Chorus* of *Vocal* and *Instrumental* Music to the Amphitheatre; where at Three o'Clock will be
An Ordinary for *Gentlemen* and *Ladies*.

About Five o'Clock, a Collection of new Songs, Ballads, Roundelays, Catches, and Glees, &c. will be performed in the *Amphitheatre*; after which the Company is desired to prepare for the Ball—which will begin exactly at Nine, with new Minuets, composed for the Occasion, and played by the whole Band.

N. B. The Steward hopes the Gentlemen and Ladies will wear the Favors

vors that are prepared on this Occasion, and called the *Shakespeare Favors.*

The whole Town of *Stratford* being informed by these Advertisements—several Guns were fired as Signals for the Morning's Entertainment—the MAGISTRATES assembled about Eight in one of the principal Streets;——Mr. GARRICK, the *Steward,* appeared at the *Town Hall,* the Place appointed for the public Breakfast, to see that every Thing was properly prepared for the Reception of the Company, and to be in readiness to receive them——but previous to the coming of the Company, the MAYOR, at the Head of the *Corporation,* in their Formalities, waited on Mr. GARRICK, and in a polite Speech, delivered by the Town Clerk, presented him with a *Medalion* of

Shake-

Shakespeare, carved on a piece of the famous *Mulberry Tree,* and richly set in Gold.— Mr. GARRICK, to this elegant mark of Distinction, made a suitable Reply—and instantly fastened it on his Breast. From the Town Hall the Company retired at half after Ten to the Church, where the ORATORIO of JUDITH was to be given, conducted by Doctor *Arne*.——When the Oratorio was over—the Steward, with a great Number of the Gentlemen, walked in Procession from the CHURCH to the AMPHITHEATRE, with all the Band of Music and Singers, in full Chorus before them—chanting the following Lines, accompanied with proper Instruments.

"This is the Day! a holyday!
"Drive Care and Sorrow far away!
"Let all be Mirth and hallow'd Joy!
"Here *Nature* nurs'd her darling Boy!
                                                "Whose

"Whose Harp the Muses strung!
"From Heart to Heart let Raptures bound!
"Now, now, we tread enchanted Ground,
"Here *Shakespeare* walk'd and sung!"

At the AMPHITHEATRE at three o'Clock—an elegant Dinner was served for six or seven hundred Gentlemen and Ladies.—And when Dinner was over, the Band of Music and Singers appeared in the Orchestra, and entertained the Company with Ballads, Catches, and Glees—'till it was time to retire to new dress and prepare for the Ball—between nine and ten the Company began to repair thither—and in that short Interval, a great number of Hands were employed to decorate and illuminate the AMPHITHEATRE.——When Night approached, the Inhabitants of *Stratford* testified their Joy by lighting up every Window in every House, and every House in every Street in the Town. This made the Night as chearful as the Day—the Affembly was crowded and brilliant; the Ball opened foon after ten, and the Country Dances continued till three o'Clock in the Morning.

SECOND DAY.

The STEWARD of the JUBILEE informs the Company that at nine o'Clock will be a

PUBLIC BREAKFAST,

at the TOWN HALL.

At Eleven o'Clock, a PAGEANT, (if the Weather will permit) to proceed from the *College* to the *Amphitheatre*,

Where An ODE

(upon dedicating a BUILDING and erecting a STATUE to the Memory of SHAKE-SPEARE) will be performed, after which the PAGEANT will return to the *College*.

At Four an Ordinary for *Ladies* and Gentlemen.

At Eight, the Fire-Works.

And at Eleven o'Clock,

The Masquerade.

The Town Hall was crouded, as before, at Breakfast—but the Morning proving rainy, the most showy Part of the Entertainment (particularly for the Country People, the Young and Gay) I mean the Pageant, was obliged to be omitted. —But the more sensible Part of the Company, who promised themselves more Pleasure from Poetry and Music, from *Sense* and *Sound* united—they hastened to secure good Places at the Amphitheatre, to the Performance of the Ode! Mr. *Garrick* (the Author of the Ode) appeared in the Front-line, with the female Singers on each Side of him, and (after the Overture)

ture) spoke the Recitative Parts, which had so great an Effect, that, perhaps, in all the Characters he ever played, he never shewed more Powers, more Judgment, or ever made a stronger Impression on the Minds of his Auditors! And though he was frequently disturbed by the turbulence of Applause, it was *then*, generally allowed by all I heard speak of it, that the ODE, in point of *poetical Merit*, and the SPEAKER, in point of *Elocution*, were justly intitled to universal Admiration!

It should therefore be remarked in this Place, that Mr. *Garrick* was the first who conceived the Idea of speaking the Recitative, which in general is the most languid and neglected Part of a musical Performance; if his Example were followed, and good Speakers could be procured, the happy Mixture of fine Speaking and Music, fic, would afford a moſt exquiſite and rational Entertainment.

Mr. *Garrick*, in the Performance of this Ode, diſtinguiſhed himſelf equally as a *Poet*, an *Actor*, and a *Gentleman*;—and when it was over, he lamented in a proſe Addreſs to his Auditors, that none of the eminent Poets of our Univerſities had undertaken the Subject, who were infinitely more capable than himſelf, to execute that arduous Taſk.—He expreſſed an Apprehenſion, that his Zeal for the Honour of *Shakeſpeare* had led him to expoſe the weakneſs of his own Abilities; but hoped his Motive would apologize for his Defects:—then turning to Doctor *Arne*, he politely added, that the firſt muſical Genius in this Country, did not think his Muſe unworthy the Exerciſe of his Talents, and that he was certain the Compoſer's Excellence would amply attone for the Imperfections of the Author.

He added, that he now perceived too late, the wide Difference between speaking in public, supported by the Genius of *Shakespeare*, and celebrating that Genius, supported only by his own weak Abilities; —but as this is his *first Attempt in this Way*, he hopes for that Favour and Indulgence which is always given to every Stage Adventurer, who appears for the first Time in any Character.

May he not hope too, that his weak Endeavours will be supported by those (whom he has the Honour to see before him) who having Powers equal to it, will do Justice to a Subject the most worthy of their Admiration, and their Eloquence.

——Hear what our *English Homer* says,

" What

" What need my SHAKESPEARE, for his honour'd
" bones,
" The Labour of an Age in piled Stones;
" Or that his hallow'd Reliques should be hid,
" Under a Star-y pointing Pyramid!
" Dear Son of Memory, great Heir of Fame!
" What need'st thou such weak witness of thy Name!
" *Thou*, in our Wonder and Astonishment,
" Hast built thyself a live-long Monument!
" And so sepulcher'd, in such Pomp dost lie,
" That *Kings* in such a Tomb, would wish to die!

If you want still a greater Authority than MILTON's, for the unequalled Merits of SHAKESPEARE, consult your own Hearts—I would not pay them so ill a Compliment to suppose, that he has not made a dear, valuable, and lasting Impression upon them!——Your *Attendance here* upon this Occasion, is a Proof that you felt—powerfully felt his Genius! and that you love and revere him and his Memory:

—the only remaining Honour to him now (and it is the greateſt Honour you can do him) is to SPEAK for him.—

[Here a Pauſe enſued with a general Laugh]——
Perhaps my Propoſition (continued he) comes a little too abruptly upon you? with your Permiſſion, we will deſire theſe Gentlemen [the Band of Muſic] to give you time, by a Piece of Muſic, to recollect and adjuſt your Thoughts.

[After the Piece of Muſic]
Now, Ladies and Gentlemen, will you be pleaſed to ſay any Thing *for*, or *againſt* SHAKESPEARE?

Upon this Mr. KING, ſo juſtly celebrated for his comic Talents, roſe up from amongſt the Auditors, in the Character of a MACARONI, being well dreſſed, or diſguiſed for the Purpoſe, and accepted the Propoſal Mr. *Garrick* had made—On being invited

invited to the *Orchestra*, he there declared he had many Exceptions to make against *Shakespeare*. He complained of his being a vulgar Author, only capable of exciting those vulgar Emotions of laughing and crying.—That it was the Criterion of a Gentleman to be moved at nothing—to feel nothing—to admire nothing.——He owned that he did not much love his Country—yet he could wish that it would submit to be civilized—and as the first Step to it, never to suffer so execrable a fellow as *Shakespeare*, with his *Things*, which are called *Tragedies* and *Comedies*, to debauch their Minds, and Understandings, and produce *Snivelings* and *Horse-laughs*—when the chief Excellence of Man, and the most refined Sensation, was to be devoured by *Ennui*, and only live in a State of insensible Vegetation.—Then he threw out his Sarcasms against the *Jubilee*, the *Steward*, the *Corporation*, and all the *Company*, which occasioned Mirth, and gave a great Variety to the Entertainment.

After he had done, the *Steward* said, I must beg Leave in the Name of all the Admirers of *Shakespeare*, to return our Thanks to that very fine and refined Gentleman and Critic, for the great *Panegyric* he has been pleased to bestow upon their Favourite.

O Ladies! it is you, and you alone can put a Stop to this terrible Progress and Irruption of these *Anti-Goths* (as they are pleased to call themselves). *It was you, Ladies,* that restored SHAKESPEARE to the Stage! You formed yourselves into a Society to protect his Fame! and erected a MONUMENT to HIS and YOUR OWN HONOUR in WESTMINSTER ABBEY! He
has

has been always supported in his universal Dominion by his fair Admirers!—and his Throne has been established in their Smiles and Tears.——Therefore as that *lovely Sex* and the *Poet* have mutually admired, and defended each other, I shall address myself to them in particular to protect their *Bard* from every Attack of those, who having refined away their Feelings, must have lost their Taste for NATURE, BEAUTY, and SHAKESPEARE.

[To the LADIES.]

" In these strange Times of Party and Division,
" Why should not I amongst the rest *petition?*
" In *Shakespeare*'s Name I invocate the Fair!
" Whilst on my Breast their Patron Saint I wear—
      [shews the Medal.]
" He LOV'D the Sex—not like your Men of Prose,
" Or common Bards, whose Blood but ebbs and flows;
" His Love was Rapture—of superior Note.
" *Shakespeare* could only love as *Shakespeare* wrote—
        " If

" If here, and there, perhaps he ſtains his Page,
" (And there are Prodigies in every Age)
" If he paints female Characters, whoſe Crimes,
" Belie the Sex, and ſtartle modern Times——
" He brands them Monſters, with his pow'rful Pen!
" Nay, makes them like his Witches—almoſt Men!
" O naughty *Man! you* are to blame alone;
" Yours are their Faults, their Virtues all their own:
" The *Foibles* of the Fair, when *Shakeſpeare* draws,
" He ſpecious Motives finds for ſeeming Flaws:
" Does *Lady Ann* from ſtrict Decorum part,
" Poor Soul—it was her Tenderneſs of Heart:
" Then 'twas a MONARCH woo'd!—and where
 " are they
" (Except this Company) of mortal Clay,
" Who would reſiſt a CORONATION Day?
" To ſooty Arms if *Deſdemona* flies——
" *Black Men are Pearls in beauteous Ladies Eyes*—
" And what's a Shade of Blackneſs more or leſs?
" The Damſel run away we muſt confeſs——
" Left her old Father—but that Fault is rare,
" She was of *Venice* too—a warmer Air——
" For *Engliſh* Ladies only will I ſwear.

         " But

" But who made her so frail—so pure before ?—
" Why *he*, the naughty Man, the Blackamoor.
" Guard well your Hearts, ye Fair, from Love's
   " Attack——
" There are all Sorts of Devils, white and black—
" When *Juliet*, Hero, *Imogen*, he drew,
" And sprightly *Rosalind*, he dreamt of *you!*
" Whate'er of *Wit*, of *Grace*, or *Fancy* flow'd,
" *Shakespeare* on *you*, his best, lov'd Theme bestow'd!
" 'Twas *you* engross'd his first, his fond Regard,
" And you, to Nature just, revere the *Bard*-——
" Spite of all Malice—here I glorying stand—
" That *Shakespeare*'s Tree produc'd this little * Wand:
" From *this* to me, such Heart-felt Transport springs,
" As *Staffs* to *Gen'rals*, *Scepters* give to *Kings!*
" The *Parent Tree* from whence its Life it drew,
" Beneath his Care, its earliest Culture knew,
" And with his Fame, the spreading Branches grew.
" How once it flourish'd feeling Crowds can tell ;
" Unfeeling Foes will mention how it fell :
" Nor let us wonder how such Things can be ;
" The infect Vermin fly-blow every Tree.

   * Made of the *Mulberry Tree*.

" The

" The Name of *Shakespeare* ever will be dear—
" While *Joy* shall smile—and *Sorrow* drop the Tear;
" While *Beauty* charms, *he* charms—not only You,
" Whom now the Glory of this Day we view!
" Your Daughters Daughters shall confess his Pow'r,
" Till language fail, or Time shall be no more;
" Shall on his Cause enraptur'd Judges sit,
" And *Beauty* ever prove, the *Patroness of Wit.*

Thus, as *Pope* says, was *this Feast of Reason, and the Flow of Soul*, never enjoyed with more Rapture than was testified by every Auditor! Every Friend congratulating each other on the Pleasure he had received.

But the Dinner Bell began soon to summon them to feast on Sensualities.——At Four o'Clock a Turtle was to be served up, of an hundred and fifty Pounds weight, which, with a number of other Dainties, and rich Wines, was only a proper Entertainment for the splendid Company assembled there!

At

At Eight o'Clock a very expenfive and curious *Fire-work* was erected on the other Side the *Avon*, under the Direction of Mr. *Angelo*—but the heavy Rain that fell about that Time, entirely deftroyed that Exhibition.

The Company being difappointed of that Pleafure, were obliged to return to their Lodgings, to prepare for the MASQUE-RADE, which was appointed at *Eleven* that Night, and was greatly crouded.—All the *Nobility* and *principal Gentry*, who carried their own Dreffes thither, were very fplendid—but thofe who had not that Advantage, paid dearly for *Habits* brought by the Dealers of *London*, to a *public Mafquerade*, near an hundred Miles diftant.——— Among the moft diftinguifhed Characters in this Affembly was Lady *Pembroke*—Mrs. *Bouverie*, and Mrs. *Crew*—habited like

like *Witches*—The Contrast between the *Deformity* of the *feigned*, and the *Beauty* of the *real* Appearance—was universally admired! Lord *Grosvenor* was magnificently dressed in an Eastern Habit.——But the most remarkable Character was Mr. *Boswell*, the well-known Friend of PAOLI—He appeared in a *Corsican Habit*, with Pistols in his Belt, and a Musket at his Back—and in the Front of his Cap, in Gold Letters, were these Words, 'PAOLI and LIBERTY. Mr. *Boswell* (who had visited that General when at the Head of his *Corsican* Army, and has published an Account of that Expedition)—had wrote a short Poem, by way of Prologue, which he intended to have spoke at the *Masquerade*, but was prevented by the Crowd—the Poem has been since published in our News-Papers. The principal Personages who honoured

this

this Jubilee—were, the Duke of *Dorſet*, Lord and Lady *Hertford*, Lord *Groſvenor*, Lord *Denbigh*, Lord *Spencer*, Lord *Craven*, Lord *Beauchamp*, Duke of *Mancheſter*—Lord *Plymouth*, Lord *Carliſle*, Lord *North*, Sir *Watkins Williams Wynn*, &c.

THE THIRD DAY.

PUBLIC BREAKFAST at the TOWN HALL, at Nine o'Clock—as before—at Twelve an HORSE-RACE was appointed, for a JUBILEE-CUP of fifty Pounds Value—for which five Colts ſtarted of ſome Note on the Turf: Lord *Groſvenor*'s Colt—the Hon. Mr. *King*'s—and Mr. *Fettiplace*, Mr. *Watſon*, and *Pratt*'s Colts.—*Pratt* the Groom rode his own Colt, and won the Cup—and declared his Reſolution never to part with it, though he honeſtly confeſſed—he knew very little about *Plays*, or Maſter SHAKESPEARE.

At their Return from the *Race*, the Company repaired to the AMPHITHEATRE to Dinner;—the *French Horns* and *Clarinetts* attending—from thence to their Lodgings to dress for the BALL at Night, which was opened at Nine o'Clock:—this Evening (being fair Weather) there was a grand FIREWORK play'd off before the AMPHITHEATRE—which closed the most splendid JUBILEE that ever was *plan'd or executed* in ENGLAND; and which gave Birth to a Dramatic Representation of it at the THEATRE, that gave Delight to Ninety-two crouded Audiences that Season.

P. S. I forgot to mention that there was a STATUE of SHAKESPEARE fixed in the Front of the *Orchestra* at the *Amphitheatre*, which had a very good Effect; and after the JUBILEE it was placed in a Nich of the TOWN-HALL:—This also

was

was another Present of Mr. GARRICK's to the *Corporation of Stratford.*

I cannot quit this Subject without observing, the scandalous Behaviour of the very *low People* of the Town of *Stratford*, in regard to their *Avarice*, and shameful *Extortions*; as well as their absurd Notions relating to the *Jubilee.* They were, in general, much dissatisfied, and greatly afraid of Mischief—they had not the least Comprehension of *what,* or about *whom* such Preparations were making.—They looked upon Mr. *Garrick* as a *Magician*, who could, and would raise the Devil! And, instead of being delighted with the approaching *Festival,* many of them kept at home; and were afraid to stir abroad.— They were confirmed in their Absurdities by the black Looks and secret Operations of those who were employed in making the

the *Fireworks*—and looked on the heavy Rains that fell during the *Jubilee*, as a Mark of Heaven's Anger. In short, their Desire to get Money, and their Terrors left they should deal with the Devil, occasioned great Mirth to many of the Neighbours, and Gentlemen who delight in Humour and Pleasantry.

The Author of the *Jubilee* (as it was acted at the *Theatre Royal* in *Drury-Lane*) has opened his Farce with a Scene that ridicules (without the least Exaggeration) the unaccountable Notions, and absurd Apprehensions of the lower People of *Stratford*.— It seems as if *Providence* had created *Shakespeare* to shew what Wonders the intellectual Powers of Man might perform! and by having bestowed so much upon one of that *Town*, was resolved to take away all Ideas from three-fourths of the rest of the Inhabitants.

F I N I S.

www.ingramcontent.com/pod-product-compliance
Lightning Source LLC
Chambersburg PA
CBHW031738230426
43669CB00007B/396